MW00343198

Fun Soccer Drills that Teach Soccer Skills to 5, 6, and 7 year olds

By Alanna Jones

Rec Room Publishing LLC

––––––––––––––––––

Lusby, MD
1-888-325-GAME
www.gamesforsoccer.com

Illustrations by Alanna Jones
Cover design by Artmil
Edited by RK Edit

Copyright © 2011 by Alanna Jones

All rights reserved. No part of this publication may be reproduced or copied without written permission from the author.

Library of Congress Control Number: 2011901289
ISBN-13: 978-0-9662341-4-5

To my Dad, the hardest working and best soccer coach my friends and I ever had. Soccer was just one of the many ways we spent time together and I treasure the memories I have with you.

Contents

Introduction

Soccer is a popular game for young children to play and for good reason; everyone is involved and the basic skills are easy for five-year olds to pick up. Many soccer clubs across the country are now going to smaller sided games with as few as six players on the field at a time. This makes for a great learning environment for young players, not least since it gives each child a chance to gain more touches on the ball during the game.

Although designed for use with younger players, many of the drills in this book can be used with older, more advanced players as well. I hope you find this book easy to use and useful as you coach the great game of soccer to a new group of players just starting out or to a team that has been playing soccer together for a while.

Tips on running a great practice

Time frame
For the 5-7 year-old age group; practicing about 45 minutes to 1 hour.

Equipment
Each player should have a ball for every practice. A good equipment bag for the coach contains several disc cones, some regular cones, and colored practice vests (for dividing up the teams).

Focus on one main skill for each practice
When planning your practice, select one main topic to focus on for the day, such as dribbling, passing, or defending; all your drills should focus on this one skill. Start with the most basic drill and then

advance to more complicated drills. By focusing on only one skill, you can teach the basics; you will see improvement in the players and a better understanding of what you are trying to teach for the day. That said, some skills (such as throw-ins) warrant less focus, unless you incorporate other skills into that practice such as trapping, getting open for the ball, and passing into space when the player receives the throw-in.

Allow for maximum touches on the ball

To increase ball foot-skills, it should be your goal to make sure that each player gets as many touches on the ball as possible. Minimize and limit the amount of time players stand in line waiting. If the drill requires a line and you have a large team, break it into smaller groups. Have an assistant or parent work with one group while you work with another.

Selecting Drills

Chapters are based on specific skills. Many of the drills focus on more than one skill, as noted in the "Skills" section of each drill. Sometimes you will be working on more than one skill (i.e., during a dribbling drill players may be acting as defenders while also challenging the dribbler). However, remember to focus on teaching only one skill for each practice and to give teaching tips only about that one skill.

Plan more than you have time for

When coaching a young team, with children who have a short attention span, you need a variety of options. You have to be prepared to change to a new drill when you can see the children have lost interest or when something simply isn't working. With several drills on a list you can quickly refer to, you'll have an essential 'back up plan' for when you need to move on.

Limit the amount of time talking

Explain the drill by demonstrating. Don't give *too much* instruction. Give the kids one thing at a time to focus on. If you give them more than this they won't easily remember *any* of the things you said.

Limit the amount of time you scrimmage

During a scrimmage, one ball has to be shared by every player. During drills, each player can have maximum touches on the ball to work on his or her skills.

Fitness should be done with a ball

Practice time is short. To maximize your coaching time, do any fitness type of work with a ball and, better yet, make it a game. For example, when running a lap run while dribbling a ball, the coach also dribbles a ball at the end of the line at a slow consistent pace. If the coach isn't the last one to complete the lap, everyone has to do another lap or sing a crazy song or something similar.

If something is difficult, encourage players to slow it down

When teaching a skill, there will be a speed that each player can manage when doing it correctly and a speed that exceeds difficult. For example when teaching dribbling, encourage the players to go as slow as necessary to do it correctly. Once they master the technique at a slow speed, encourage them to step it up and go faster the next time.

Use practice to break bad habits

Children often begin playing soccer at a very young age where kicking every ball with the toe is common. Most players will continue to kick with their toe, but you should still teach correct kicking techniques so they do not form bad habits that are difficult to break as they get older. Eventually they will start to 'get it'. Be patient. It can take several seasons of play before some succeed. But, taught correctly at an early age, they will eventually develop the skills. Don't worry about them using these bad habits in the games, but, during practice, do work on breaking these habits.

Competition is good

In our culture where everyone is a "winner," young children sometimes do not do well in competitive games with a winner and loser; even so, you can incorporate an element of competition to make the drills more fun and make the players want to try harder. If the losing team has to sing a song or do the likes of a silly dance, it makes the game more enjoyable, as long as the coach approaches it in a spirit of fun. And the coach should make sure that the same players are not always the ones on the losing side.

If a drill is designed so that players get "out," make it so they can quickly get back in

Some games call for players to go out when their ball is kicked out or when they get scored on, but if the drill is designed so that the player can get back in by doing a quick exercise, he or she will be getting fit and be able to rejoin the game quickly.

Remember winning teams often have natural athletes – focus on skills, not winning

Young children develop at different speeds, and sometimes a child can be 11 months older than the youngest player on the team and have a huge advantage at these young ages. As a coach it can be discouraging to lose every game, but in the younger age groups, the teams with natural and more mature athletes are often the teams that are winning. During the games focus on using skills taught during the week and not so much on the number of goals scored; emphasize this as your focus for parents worried about their 5-year-old having a winning season. At 12-years old, the basics learned when young matters far more than how many points their team scored.

Stay Positive!

When learning soccer, young players especially need praise and encouragement. Find the small things each individual is doing well and point these small things out to foster a sense of accomplishment and pride. As an example of how to give praise while also adding feedback to help a player improve, say something like, "I like how you were _____, and if you add _____ you may find it becomes easier."

Teach a love for the game

One of your many jobs as coach is to teach soccer skills in a way that is fun and that fosters a love for the great game of soccer.

Warm Up

The main focus of a warm up drill is to get the young players focused on soccer and excited about coming to practice, while at the same time getting their muscles warmed up. The best drill to start practice is one where your players can join in easily even if the drill is already under way. This can be as simple as two people passing a ball back and forth, or something more complex that involves dribbling through cones and shooting on goal. By having a drill already in progress when practice starts, the coach has more opportunity to give individual instruction to those who show up early; it also encourages everyone to be on time. Some drills in this chapter can be used for starting out as your team shows up, while other drills will be better if started once everyone has arrived.

Warm Up Drills

Go and Get It!

Skills
Passing
Running
Dribbling

Drill Description
Each player has a ball for this drill. The team gathers into a large circle surrounding the coach, who is in the middle of a soccer field or large open area. The coach calls out the name of one of the players who passes her ball to the coach who then kicks it far out into the field in any direction. The player must run to the ball and dribble it back to the circle; meanwhile, the coach continues to call out names and receive passes and kick them out into the field. Done quickly enough, the players should be returning to the circle just in time for the coach to call their name again!

Coaching Tips
Players like this game and it's a good one to start with because it's easy for late players to join in. To encourage accurate passing, leave any ball that is not passed directly to your feet and move on to another player while waiting for the passer of the stray ball to retrieve her ball and return to her spot to pass it to you again.

Soccer Obstacle Course Chase

Skills
Varied

Drill Description
Make an obstacle course that requires players to run, dribble, kick, and throw-in. You might even use coaches or parents for different sections of the course where the players have to dribble around, kick to, etc. Set the team up in a line with your fastest players first. Give each person the same amount of head start before sending the next person. Challenge the players to catch up to, and to pass the person in front of them when going through the course.

Coaching Tips
If you set the course up in a large area with plenty of space between each obstacle the players will get lots of exercise during this drill. This is a good time for a coach to observe the techniques of individual players to see what skills the team needs to work on the most.

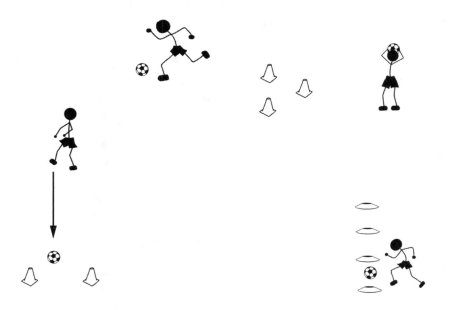

Soccer Simon Says

Skills
Varied

Drill Description
Each person should have a ball for this activity. The Coach is "Soccer Simon." Soccer Simon gives commands to the players (i.e., jump over your ball, do 10 jumping jacks, give the coach a "high five," drop kick your ball and go get it, etc.). If at any time the command is given without saying "Soccer Simon says…," those who performed the task are tricked by Soccer Simon and must do an additional task requested by the coach. This might be something like running to a tree and back, doing five sit ups, singing a silly song, or anything else that isn't so much fun that they all want to do it, yet not so awful that they feel bad when they have to do it.

Coaching Tips
The same players are often the same ones to get tricked over and over again; if this happens, allow these players to try and trick the other players by becoming "Soccer Simon."

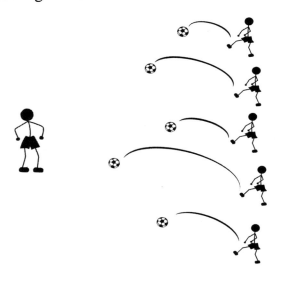

Fun Soccer Drills that Teach Soccer Skills

Follow the Coach

Skills
Varied

Drill Description
Each player lines up in single file with a ball behind the coach, who also has a ball. The coach leads the team around the field while doing several soccer-related things with the ball (i.e., dribbling, kicking, throw-ins, etc.) or funny things (i.e., run while holding the ball on top of your head, touch your elbow to the ball, sit on your ball, etc.). At any time the coach can quickly turn around and, if he finds any player who is not following the action, then the coach gets one point; if all of the players are following the direction, then the team gets a point. At the end of the activity if the coach has more points than the team does then the whole team must do an exercise, silly song, or whatever the coach requests. If the team accumulates more points than the coach, they get to think of something silly or an exercise for the coach to do.

Variation
Play *follow the leader* with different commands, and the last player to follow the command must go to the end of the line. You may allow the player in the front of the line to take three turns calling out commands before going to the end of the line and trying to work his way back to the front.

Coaching Tips
Talk about the ready stance of lightly bouncing on the balls of your feet with legs slightly bent, and have the players show you they are ready before starting this drill. Between tasks, you might want to yell "ready stance."

Race to the Ball, Race to the Coach

Skills
Getting to the ball first

Drill Description
Use one ball for this activity. The coach punts or kicks the ball out into the field and all players race to the ball. The first one to reach the ball must dribble it back to the coach while the rest of the team turns and races back. The person who got the ball then gets to kick it out the next time.

Variations
The coach kicks it out every time, but always in a different direction so that different people are closer to the ball when it is kicked and have a better chance of getting to it first.

As a reward, the first person in the racing group to make it back to you can sit out one round, etc.

The coach kicks the ball from the goal and then acts as a goalie for the person who got to the ball first. If a goal is made, the shooter gets to kick the next ball out into the air and act as goalie.

Coaching Tips
To ensure that the same kids are not always last you may run around as they try to race back to you so you are harder to get to.

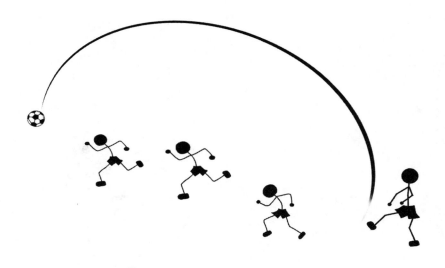

What's Next?

Skills
Varied

Drill Description
Set Up two lines at least thirty yards apart. Everyone lines up with her ball in one line. Select one player who tells everyone what they must do as they travel to the opposite line (i.e., dribble, run backwards, run while holding the ball on top of head, drop kick, etc.). After everyone makes it across the other line, select another player to decide what everyone must to do while coming back across the field. Give everyone a chance to think of something for the team to do each time.

Coaching Tips
Since each time the drill is different and kids love having control over what they get to do, this is a great drill to do over and over again at the beginning of practice.

Coach Chase

Skills
Fast running when chasing someone who has a ball

Drill Description
Starting with the ball and a three second head start, the coach begins to dribble around the practice field. The whole team chases the coach and tries to get the ball. If the team can take the ball away from the coach within one minute, then the coach has to do something, such as run a lap; if the team cannot take the ball from the coach within one minute, then they all have to run a lap (or some other activity announced before the start of this game).

Coaching Tips
Younger players think it is great fun to chase the coach. If the coach is a good dribbler, he can really wear the players out! Unless you are really good, this doesn't work for older players.

Fused

Skills
Communication
Teamwork

Drill Description
Divide the team into pairs, give each pair a ball and have the players
link arms. Give them various tasks to do while their arms are linked
together with their partner. Some possible tasks are: dribble the ball
around a cone and back together, one person dribbles down and one
person dribbles back, jump back and forth over a line, etc.

Coaching Tips
After completing the task, ask the group why it was important to
talk to each other during this drill; then ask them why it would be
important to talk to each other during a soccer game to encourage
communication.

Dribbling

Dribbling is a difficult skill for young players to master. If you can teach a young player to be a skilled dribbler, she will quickly become one of the standout players on the team.

When dribbling, the ball should be pushed out about as far as a dribbler can reach when taking a giant step. For faster dribbling the ball should be pushed out even more. For speed dribbling, the player uses the front of her foot (lower part of the laces on the front) with foot angled slightly inward. To change direction and for added control, the ball can be tapped with the inside and outside of the foot. Each person will find her own dribbling style and develop it. A skilled dribbler moves down the field with her head up so that she can see the field and make decisions about when to pass, continue dribbling, or shoot the ball. While still maintaining control, a skilled dribbler can also easily change the speed and direction of the ball when going against a defender.

One mistake young players often make is to dribble the ball too far out in front. This is done by kicking the ball and running after it while the other team can easily take the ball away. Or the player finds herself dribbling over the goal line or a touch line. Another mistake is to dribble the ball too closely. Then the player will have difficulty running or gaining speed when moving down the field.

Learning when to dribble and when not to dribble is another important part of the game of soccer. A player should dribble when there are no open teammates to pass to and when in a breakaway situation and heading toward the goal. While teaching the skill of dribbling, I often review with young players when and when not to dribble; this helps young players better make decisions when on the field for themselves.

Teaching dribbling "moves" or "fakes" is not easily done with young players, but if you can teach a young player to change her speed quickly when dribbling or to change the direction of the ball (while still maintaining control) you have taught her the first step in making a 'move'.

Shielding the ball is another important aspect of dribbling. When shielding, the player with the ball keeps her body between the defender and the ball (her back is to the defender).

When teaching dribbling to young players, a whole practice can be focused on dribbling games so that everyone has a ball at her feet for the entire practice. You may want to start with simply having the players dribble around inside of a circle to get the feel for the ball, and by challenging them to dribble with only the inside of the foot, the outside, or just the left foot or right or to alternate back and forth before starting any of the fun drills that are found in this chapter.

Dribbling Drills

Pass the Player

Skills
Quick and controlled dribbling
Out running other players

Drill Description
Set up the cones as a large circle at least ten yards in diameter. Everyone spreads out around the circle and is without a ball for the first round. Let the group know which direction to run, and on the "go" signal everyone runs around the outside of the cones and tries to pass as many other players as he can. Each time someone passes another person he yells out a number counting how many people he passes. After one minute yell "stop" and have everyone announce the number of people they have passed. After doing this once without soccer balls, have everyone get a ball and do the same drill while dribbling.

Variations
Half of the players dribble a ball while the other half runs without a ball. Those who do not have a ball try to pass those who do, and keep track of how many they pass.

Divide the group into pairs and have partners start out on opposite sides of the circle from each other. Both partners run in the same direction, and the one with a ball tries to dribble as many laps as possible without getting tagged by his partner. Once a player is tagged, the pair starts over and switches places with each other.

Coaching Tips
This is a great drill for demonstrating the need for controlled dribbling. Players who have less control will end up far wide of the circle and easily get passed on the inside by teammates who are dribbling in control.

Dribbling Drills

Continuous Circle

Skills
Dribbling with control

Drill Description
Set up a large circle using cones, with enough space between each
cone for players to dribble in and out. To create the circle, use four
more cones than there are players. Divide the group into two teams
and place one team on one half of the circle with each player standing
next to a cone and with a ball. The other team does the same on the
opposite side of the circle. There should be two empty cones between
each team on both sides. On the "go" signal, the last person in line
on each team must dribble in and out of each of her teammates until
finding the empty cone to stand by (both teams should be going in the
same direction). As soon as the dribbler reaches an empty cone she
stops and the last person on her team can go. Each team is trying to
catch up to the other team.

Variations
Instead of dribbling in and out of the cones, the last player dribbles
around the outside of the circle to the empty cone at the front of the
line. Once she gets to the cone the next player can go.

For added fun you can give the players in the line a task to do such as
jumping up and down on one foot or running in place.

Coaching Tips
This one can be difficult for younger children to figure out, so it's a
good idea to specifically tell them where to stand after they have gone
through the line.

Dribble Big Wind Blows

Skills
Dribbling while looking up

Drill Description
Make a circle out of cones with enough space between each cone for one player to stand. Make one less space than there are participants. Each player has a ball and there should be one player standing between each cone, with one player in the middle. The person in the middle is "it" and says "The Big Wind Blows for Everyone who _____." The blank is filled in with anything that is descriptive of the players in the group. "It" might say "everyone who is wearing blue," "who is six years old," "who had cereal for breakfast," etc. Anyone who fits that description must leave his own spot and dribble through the middle of the circle to find another spot, and this includes the player who was "it." The one person who does not find a new spot becomes "it" for the next round.

Variation
Give the players three animals to choose from and let everyone pick one. The person in the middle says, "Everyone who is (one of the animals) and all of those who selected to be that animal trade places. Or, the person in the middle can say, "Everyone at the zoo," and then everyone has to trade places.

Coaching Tips
Some players try to be in the middle all the time because they like to be "it." Or some players are not as good dribblers as others. When either of these things happens, the coach should select who gets to be in the middle after a few rounds. Encourage players to look up when dribbling to find which spots are open and so that they do not run into other players.

Dribbling Drills

Earthquake

Skills
Moving quickly to the ball
Working together as a group

Drill Description
Set up a square big enough for everyone inside to have room to dribble freely. The players dribble around in the area, avoiding one another and avoiding the coach who puts pressure on slow moving players. When the coach yells "earthquake" everyone must leave her own ball and find a new one before the earthquake is over (after the coach counts to five). If any player has not found a new ball by the end of earthquake, then the whole team must run a lap around the square or do some other activity announced by the coach.

Variations
Use disc cones to make small triangles around the field. When the coach yells "earthquake," each player must find a triangle to stand in for safety before the count of five.

Set up cones around the outside of the square. When the coach yells "earthquake," each player must dribble around one of the cones and back into the square. No two players can dribble around the same cone.

Coaching Tips
Remind players to dribble with their head up to see where they are going and to keep the ball in control when dribbling. Also emphasize teamwork by encouraging players to quickly find a new ball when the one they want is taken by another player.

Moving Goals

Skills
Dribbling with head up
Accurate passing

Drill Description
Set up a large square about twenty by twenty yards. Half the players have balls and half do not. When the coach says "go," all players with balls dribble around inside the square while the players without balls also move around. When the coach yells "score," the players who do not have a ball stop and become a goal wherever they are, staying in one spot with their legs apart. Those with a ball try to score by passing it through the legs of anyone who has become a goal. Once a player scores on one goal he must go find another goal to score on. The coach counts to ten out loud before yelling "go" again. Do this for a few rounds and then ask the players to announce how many scores they made. After a few rounds, switch dribblers.

Variations
For added fun, give each player a unique sound they must make when someone scores a goal through their legs.

Two coaches act as a goal and run around but stop at various places in the field with either their legs spread apart for a goal or by holding hands up in the air together to make the cross bar of the goal.

Coaching Tips
Young players can't always remember how many goals they scored or they make up a number so don't make a big deal out of how many they score. But they do have fun announcing it. Encourage side of the foot passing with proper follow through. As noted, dribbling should be done with the head up to avoid a collision and so the dribblers know where the goals are.

How Many?

Skills
Dribbling with head up

Drill Description
Every player has a ball and lines up in a single file line. Announce a destination for the group to dribble to and back from. If you are at a soccer field, players can dribble laps around the field. Before they start, tell them that when they are dribbling at some point they must hold one hand off to the side or behind their backs with one through five fingers held up for a few seconds. Send them off with space in between each player and when they all return ask them to tell you how many fingers the person in front of them held up. Then ask the person who held up the fingers if they were correct. To keep a good pace and so that everyone has someone's fingers to read, the coach should run in the front of the line.

Variations
Have the group spread out in a circle, all dribbling in one direction and each one following the person in front of her.

Pair the players up with a partner and have them take turns following each other anywhere around the field while holding up fingers behind the back. Gather the group and ask how many fingers were held up before switching leaders. Encourage change of speed and direction when doing it in partners.

Coaching Tips
This is a great way to help players dribble with their head up and also to give those players who don't want to run an incentive to keep up with the group.

Dribbling Drills

Soccer Red Light Green Light

Skills
Keeping control of the ball when dribbling and being able to stop it quickly

Drill Description
Each individual has a ball and lines up on one line facing the coach, who should be at least twenty yards away. When the coach turns his back and says "green light," the players dribble towards the coach until he turns around facing them and says, "red light." At this point everyone should bring his ball to a stop. If anyone's ball rolls ahead without stopping, he is sent as far back as the last player. The game keeps going in a "red light, green light" fashion until one of the players reaches the coach and he becomes the next "it" and calls out "red light, green light."

Coaching Tips
Before starting this game, it is a good idea to practice stopping the ball quickly by placing the foot on top of the ball.

Fun Soccer Drills that Teach Soccer Skills

Mystery Finish Line

Skills
Keeping the ball close when dribbling
Changing direction quickly
Looking up when dribbling

Drill Description
Start in the middle of the field or practice area, and everyone has a ball. Look around and find something everyone can all see and say, "Dribble to the basketball hoop, tall tree, swing set, Jacob's mom (or anything else you see)." Everyone immediately dribbles toward that object until you yell something else for them to dribble toward. As soon as you announce something else, everyone should change direction. If you want to make it a race, do not let them know what the last thing is that they will be running toward because this is the ultimate end of the "race."

Coaching Tips
If there are several trees (or other objects the team is dribbling around) yell "dribble around the tree," and point to the selected tree so that players have to practice dribbling with their heads up.

Twist

Skills
Dribble with control and stopping the ball quickly

Drill Description
Form a circle with cones or use the circle from the middle of a regulation size soccer field. Everyone starts with a ball and is spread out around the outside of the circle. There are three commands: go, stop, and twist. When the coach yells "go," everyone should start dribbling around the outside of the circle in one direction until the coach yells "stop" or "twist." When the players hear "stop," each puts her foot on the top of his ball and waits for the next command. A "twist" command means quickly turn your ball and start dribbling in the other direction.

Coaching Tips
Emphasize how important it is to keep the ball close enough to your body when dribbling so that you are able to stop or turn quickly and so that the other team can't get it. You may want to review how to quickly turn the ball prior to starting the drill. The ball can be turned quickly by pulling it back with the foot on top of the ball or by reaching out and pulling the ball back under the body with the instep or outside of the foot.

Soccer Bench Ball

Skills
Shielding the ball and taking the opponent's ball
Dribbling in a small space

Drill Description
Set up the cones in a square about ten by ten yards, and everyone starts in the middle with a ball. Everyone tries to kick everyone else's ball out of the square. If your ball is kicked out, you have to remember who kicked your ball out and stand on the side and watch them. Once the person who kicked your ball out is out you get to go back in. If a player accidentally kicks his own ball out he has to do fifteen jumping jacks before returning to the game, and anyone they knocked out can come back in. For added fun you can encourage those who are out to yell "get _____ out" (filling in the blank with the person who got them out). Players like to have those on the sideline yelling for them to get out because it means they are good and able to get others out.

Coaching Tips
This is a classic game with a new twist. It helps to have the coach watching the game tell each player who got them out, so the player knows who to watch and when to go back in.

Don't Crash

Skills
Dribbling with your head up
Dribbling under control

Drill Description
Set up a narrow lane about ten feet wide and twenty yards long. Divide the team into two groups in which everyone has a ball. One group lines up on the narrow end of the lane on one side and the other group lines up across from them on the opposite side. On the "go" signal, everyone has the count of five to dribble to the other side without touching another player's ball or body with their own ball or any part of their body. Each player and her ball must also stay within the lines. After the count of five, each player who made it across and who stopped her ball on the line on the other side receives one point and gets to yell a cheer of excitement. Repeat this drill several times going back and forth.

Variations
Start with the count of ten, and then each time give the players less time to get across.

Have each player who didn't make it across without touching something do three jumping jacks or other exercise or sing a funny song.

Simply give a point to the team that reaches the other side first. (You may or may not give points to teams that make it yet have players who crash into someone or go out of bounds.)

Coaching Tips
Emphasize dribbling the ball while looking up. This enables one to avoid running into other players and to keep the ball in control to avoid upcoming obstacles.

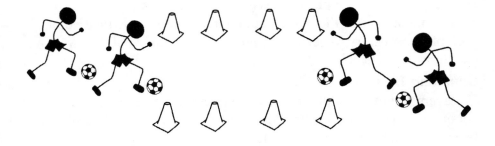

Dribble Musical Cones

Skills
Dribbling quickly

Drill Description
Make a large circle using disc cones. The circle should have one less cone than there are players. Everyone has a ball and dribbles around the outside of the circle in the same direction when the coach starts the music. This can be actual music, the coach singing or blowing a whistle to signal the start. When the music stops (or the whistle is blown again) each player must quickly find a disc cone to stop his ball on or stop it next to one. The one person who does not find a cone has to do three jumping jacks or sing a song for the next round.

Variations
Divide the group into two teams and stage the players around the circle so that every other person is from a different team. When the music stops, the members of the team of the player who did not find a cone has to do the three jumping jacks (or other activity).

For added excitement, allow players to kick another player's ball away before stopping on a cone.

Place a pile of balls in the middle of a large circle (there should be one less ball than there are players). When the music starts everyone runs around the outside of the circle until the music stops at which point each player must try to get a ball and dribble it outside of the circle.

Coaching Tips
If players want to sing the song for the next round and purposefully get out, change the drill so that they do something nobody wants to do (such as a goofy dance or sit-ups).

Dribble Around and Back Again

Skills
Dribbling with head up
Dribbling with speed

Drill Description
Set up a square big enough for everyone to dribble around in. Outside the square set up different sets of cones. One set has one cone, another has two, another three, and one set has four. The players dribble around inside the square until the coach yells a number. Players must dribble around the cones that correlate with that number and get back to the middle square. Allow the player who makes it back to the middle first to call out the number for the next round.

Variations
The last one back gets a point. The person with the most points at the end has to do a special task (exercise, sing a silly song). Or make the person with the least amount of points be "it" for the next activity if you have an appropriate drill planned.

To further emphasize dribbling with your head up, the Coach moves around and then holds up one through four fingers instead of yelling the number of cones to be dribbled around.

Yell out a simple math problem and the answer to the problem is one of the sets of cones.

Coaching Tips
If you have a slow dribbler, select the cones closest to that player to be the cones that are dribbled around. It's important to dribble with your head up and keep the ball within one step to keep it in control when dribbling in the square. When sprint dribbling, the ball can be a few steps out in front but not so far in front that the other team can get it or the player loses control.

Corner to Corner

Skills
Dribbling

Drill Description
Set up a ten yard by ten yard square with a smaller one yard square at each corner. Divide the group into two teams with one team in one corner square and the other team in another corner square. (Make sure the two teams start out next to each other with an empty small square across from each team.) Each player has a ball. When you say "go," one player from each team must dribble across the square to the opposite corner and stop the ball in that square; this player must then make a turn and return to the square she started in, and she must stop her ball before the next player in line can proceed. Since each team is doing this at the same time, they have to watch out for other dribblers in the middle. The first team with everyone dribbling from one side to the other and back is declared the winner.

Variations
Instead of taking turns, have everyone go at once. The team with everyone back in its original square is declared the winner.

Go from one sideline to the opposite, rather than from corner to corner.

Start with four teams. Each team starts in one corner of the square and all go at once to the opposite side and back, being careful not to collide in the middle when dribbling.

Coaching Tips
When there are several players in the middle at once, it really forces players to keep the ball under control; this controlled playing is better than dribbling by the kick and run method that many young players often use.

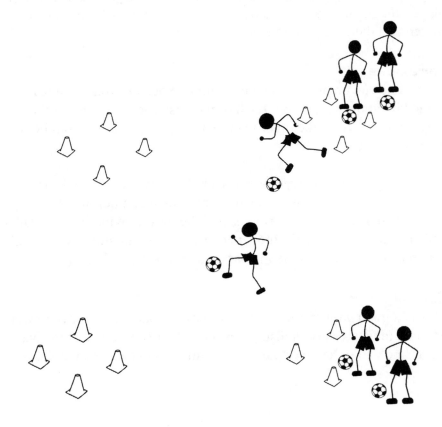

Soccer Freeze Tag

Skills
Dribbling with your head up

Drill Description
Make a large square using the cones or this game can be played in the goal box, center circle, the entire field, or other already marked off areas. Select one person to be "it." This person does not have a ball, but all of the other players do. When the coach says "go," all the players with balls dribble around the area and try to avoid being tagged. The person who is "it" can tag anyone. Once tagged, a player is "frozen" and must hold her ball over her head. If any of the other players makes a pass with their ball between the legs of a frozen player, then that person becomes unfrozen. Play until everyone is frozen and then select a new person to become 'it'.

Variations
This game can be played in teams with one person from each team being "it" at the same time. Each of the "its" tries to get all of the players frozen from the other team before all the players from her own team are frozen.

Play this game where everyone has a ball but two of the balls are "poison." If you have two balls that are a distinct color, it is best to use these balls. Everyone dribbles and the players with the "poison" balls try to kick their ball into a player's ball so that this player then becomes frozen until someone passes a ball between her legs.

Coaching Tips
This is a good game for the coach to play so that she can save players who are tagged easily; it also gives the chaser someone fast to chase for a time while the other players are unfreezing their teammates.

Tag with Bases

Skills
Quick dribbling and control

Drill Description
Set up bases around the practice area by using disc cones to form small triangles. Have a few less bases than there are players. Each player has a ball except for one who is "it." The player who is "it" tries to tag anyone dribbling a ball. Once someone is tagged they must give their ball to the person who tagged them and then the tagged player becomes "it." The bases can be used for safety from the player who is "it," but only one player can be in a base at a time; this player must have possession of his own ball and can only stay on base for the count of three. A player cannot return to the base he just left before first going to a different base.

Coaching Tips
This drill works on dribbling speed but can also present a good opportunity to point out the benefits of being spread out and not bunched together.

Fun Soccer Drills that Teach Soccer Skills

Timed Tag

Skills
Quick and controlled dribbling
Dribble and then pass

Drill Description
Set up a square ten yards by ten yards (or larger) and half of the
players (or slightly less) each have a ball. The remaining players do
not have a ball and everyone must stay inside the square. When the
game starts, those with a ball try to hit those who do not have a ball.
Once a player is hit she must take the ball that hit her and try to hit a
player with that ball. When you say "stop," everyone who has a ball
must dribble her ball to the place you specify and back before the next
round starts.

Coaching Tips
This is a fast moving game, since nobody wants to have to run in the
end. You can vary the amount of time allowed each round so that they
never know when you will say "stop" and to ensure that the same
players are not always running in the end.

Demolition Derby

Skills
Dribbling with your head up to see what's going on around you
Accurate kicking

Drill Description
Mark off a square large enough for everyone to move around in while dribbling. Everyone has a ball and begins dribbling around inside the square. As soon as the coach says, "go," everyone tries to hit everyone else with his own ball. If a player's ball goes out of the square, he can quickly go get it and rejoin the game after doing five jumping jacks. Once a player is hit, he is "out" and must leave the square. Play until one player is left in the middle.

Variation
Once a player is out, give him an exercise to do before he can return to the game.

Coaching Tips
This is a fun, fast moving drill and the players like it when the coaches play and they can chase after the coach. Also, when a coach plays he can balance the game out by going after the best players so the same people aren't the last ones in all the time. This is a another good drill to encourage dribbling with your head up.

Get to the Ball First!

Skills
Dribbling quickly
Getting to the ball quickly before the other team does without being intimidated by them

Drill Description
Divide the team into two groups and have each group line up across from each other with about ten yards between the two groups. Place a ball in the middle, between the two teams. Call out one player's name from each team and then say, "go." These two players race to the ball and try to dribble it across the other team's line. Give one "point" to the player who got the first touch on the ball and one "point" to the player who was able to get it across the other team's line.

Variations
Set up small goals for each team to score on that are on the sides; this way the players start on the "sideline" and then try to score on their designated goal.

Throw the ball into the center, rather than having it sitting there ready for them.

The players on the line may act as defenders or as goalies to try to stop the player from dribbling across their line.

Coaching Tips
This drill is useful for encouraging players to not back down when running to the ball while an opponent is also running to the ball. Some players are more timid than others and will let the other team get the ball when they could have actually been the one to get it.

Circle Dribble Race

Skills
Dribbling quickly
Dribbling with head up to avoid obstacles

Drill Description
Set up a large circle using small disc cones. For each two players set up one larger cone on the outer edge of the circle, and evenly space these cones around the circle. Each player has a ball and is paired with a partner. Each player stands back to back with her partner by one of the large cones, and on the "go" signal both dribble in opposite directions and try to both make it back to their cone before the other teams make it back to their own cones. The first team back wins and gets a point. After a few rounds of this, each player has to find her partner when dribbling around the circle and swap balls before continuing on to their cone.

Coaching Tips
This is a real running game that will help get your team in shape. Emphasize dribbling with your head up to see who is coming at you and to avoid crashing into other players. Switch partners around if one team is dominating too much or, just for fun, halfway though so that they won't be able to tell who really won.

Dribble Kickball

Skills
Dribbling quickly

Drill Description
Set up a kickball field and for bases use cones to make squares that can be dribbled into. Divide the group into two teams with one team in the outfield and one team kicking. The players on the kicking team should each have a ball and the outfield should have one ball. The pitcher makes a nice pass to the first kicker who kicks the ball into the outfield and then dribbles another ball around the bases. A player is safe if he stops his ball inside one of the base squares. The outfield cannot use hands and must get to the ball and control it. The outfield can get a player "out" if one of them can dribble the ball into the square before the dribbler gets there. Another way to get a player out is to dribble the ball that was kicked and chase after a player (one who is off of a base) and tag them by hand as the player is running. You can play "three outs" before switching who is up. Or you can have everyone get a chance to kick once before switching.

Coaching Tips
This is a fun game to end practice with after working on dribbling skills.

Hospital

Skills
Quick dribbling
Dribbling and then kicking accurately

Drill Description
Divide the group into two teams and everyone has a ball. Make a small square at one end of the field and one at the other end about twenty yards apart. Select one player from each team to be that team's Doctor and give them a ball and have each Doctor go stand in a different square (the hospital). When you say "go," everyone finds a ball and can dribble anywhere in the playing area while trying to kick a ball at someone on the other team and hit that player from the knee down. Once a player is hit she must freeze with her hands above her head to signal to her team's Doctor that she is frozen and needs to be healed. The Doctor must dribble to the player and touch her with the ball she is dribbling with before returning back to the hospital. When a Doctor is in the hospital she is safe, but once she comes out of the hospital the other team can get her "out," and when a Doctor gets "out" her team loses the game. Select two new Doctors every time a team loses, and start a new game.

Coaching Tips
This game requires a great deal of running and is a fun game to end practice with when the kids are tired but will still be motivated by the competition found in a fun game.

Dribbling Drills

Going Through Gates

Skills
Dribbling in control

Drill Description
Set up several small gates around the field, using two cones to make each gate. Everyone has a ball for this drill and, in one minute, each player tries to dribble through as many gates as possible without going through the same gate twice.

Variations
Break the group into pairs. While one partner is dribbling, his partner is counting how many gates he goes through in one minute. Then switch.

Instead of dribbling, have pairs pass a ball through each gate with a partner.

Coaching Tips
The better the players the smaller the gates should be. Do this drill more than once and challenge players to try to go through more gates the second time than they did the first.

Around the Object

Skills
Dribbling quickly with control

Drill Description
Select something around the practice field (trees, adults, playground balls, etc.). Say a number and tell the team what you have selected and they have to dribble the ball around this but they don't have to all go to the same one at the same time. You might say, "dribble around five trees and come back to me". Each player has to find any five trees in the area, and dribble around each one before returning to the coach. It helps if they count out loud as they go around each object.

Coaching Tips
This is a good drill for getting players into shape. A lot of running can be required, depending on what is selected for the players to run around. Emphasize proper dribbling technique of keeping one's head up and keeping the ball close enough to the body to keep it under control; yet, as long as it is still under control, the ball can also be kicked out in front of the player for sprinting.

Passing

It's a major accomplishment when a team of young players move from "bunch ball" soccer (where everyone chases after the ball and tries to kick it), and is transformed to a team of players who pass the ball. Learning how to make a proper pass is the first step toward creating a passing team.

Younger players will often kick with their toe and then follow through by stepping across the non-kicking foot and end up cross legged, which makes for an uncontrolled pass. Another passing mistake at this age is that the ball is kicked too hard or too soft, making it difficult for the kicker's teammate to receive the ball.

When making a proper pass, the inside of the foot is used to kick the ball. The non-kicking foot should be placed beside the ball and pointed in the direction the kicker wishes the ball to go. When kicking, the non-kicking leg is slightly bent and beside the ball; the kicking foot faces out with the toe up with the ankle locked, with shoulders and hips facing square to the target. The inside of the foot should make contact with the middle of the ball, or slightly above the middle of the ball, and the heel of the kicking foot should rotate in the direction of the target during the kick. After making contact with the ball the foot should remain in the same stiff position with a follow through of the leg swing.

The outside of the foot can also be used to make a pass with the same stance as used for the inside of the foot pass but with the toe of the kicking foot pointed down and in, with the ankle locked. The ball is hit with the outside of the foot.

Knowing when to pass and when to hang onto the ball and dribble are important aspects of teaching young players about passing.

Players should pass when facing pressure from the opposing team to a teammate who is open for a pass. Players should also be encouraged to pass if a teammate is closer to the goal than they are and not covered by a defender. These are not the only times it is best to pass the ball, but for young players it is best to keep it simple and give them only a few "rules" to learn so that they can make the best decisions when on the field.

Knowing where to pass is another important skill you can teach. The ball should be played in front of a player who is running down the field; this way the receiver can run onto the ball and collect it on the run, rather than having to stop and wait for a ball that has been passed to him. This is often referred to as passing into space.

Receiving a pass
Trapping a moving ball is a skill that can be taught along with passing. When a ball is passed to a player, he should first move to meet the ball. He should cushion the ball with his foot (he can also use his thigh, chest, or head for air balls) by allowing the ball to hit his foot and then, for a cushioning effect, move his foot back as the ball hits it. A skilled player will be able to trap it with just enough cushion to stop the ball, but places it slightly in front so that he can easily transition from receiving the ball to dribbling, passing or shooting. Many young players will want to step on top of the ball to stop it. This is an effective way to stop the ball, but makes the transition to running or kicking the ball difficult.

Passing Drills

Pass Pattern

Skills
Passing
Communication when passing

Drill Description
The team stands in a circle and the coach, also a part of the circle, starts with a pile of soccer balls. The coach passes to one person and calls out the player's name. This person passes to someone else and calls out her name, and must remember the person she passes to. This continues until everyone has been passed to and the last person sends the ball back to the coach. The coach then starts by passing one ball to the person she passed to the first time. This ball goes through to all the players in the same order as before. The coach then adds one more ball at a time until there are several balls being passed at a time.

Coaching Tips
Encourage players – by calling the receiving player's name out first and making eye contact – to wait for the person receiving the pass to show she is ready to receive the pass. When several balls get going at once it becomes clear without looking who is just kicking; and who is making sure her teammate is ready to receive the pass.

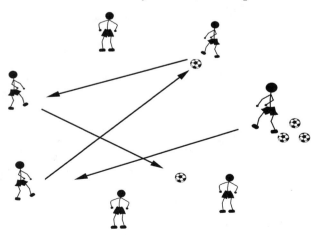

All of Your Team

Skills
Varied

Drill Description
Divide the group into pairs and have them pass back and forth with their partners until you yell, "All (your team name)…" and give a command that everyone must do. You might have them hop to a tree, run to the goal post, skip around the coach or anything else you can think of. After completing the task, each person must get back together with his partner and continue passing back and forth until the next command.

Variation
Give "points" to the team that makes it back together first after each command.

Coaching Tips
Walk around when players are in pairs so that they must be aware of where you are as well as pay attention to the partner.

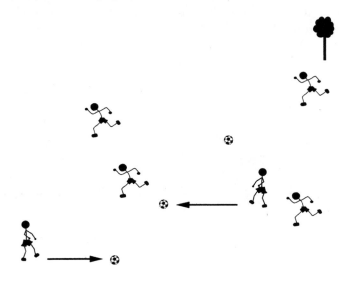

Through the Legs Passing

Skills
Accurate passing

Drill Description
Divide the group into pairs and give each pair one ball. One partner starts with the ball while her partner is about ten feet away with her legs spread apart to create a small goal which her partner tries to kick the ball through. The receiver then fetches the ball and does the same. Have each team count out loud every time they get a pass through the legs of their partner for a little friendly competition and to see which team scores more points before the coach yells "stop."

Variation
Set up two cones about three feet apart in between each player and their partner. Each team scores one "point" each time the pass is through the cones. This variation emphasizes trapping as well as accurate passing but isn't quite as fun.

Coaching Tips
Emphasize side of the foot passing and only give points when a proper pass has been made.

Individual Cone Knock Over

Skills
Accurate passing

Drill Description
Set up several small squares using the disc cones that are about two yards across. In the middle of each square place a single cone. Each player has a ball and dribbles up to a square and tries to knock the cone over by kicking their ball into it without going inside the square. After attempting to knock one cone over they must go to another square. If a cone is knocked over the player who knocked it over must set it back up before moving on to another square. Players try to get as many points as they can before the coach says "stop".

Coaching Tips
Young players will often dribble and then when they stop to pass or shoot will take a step back before kicking the ball. Encourage players to dribble and pass at the cones without backing up. I often tell players to "flick it and kick it" if they need to give it an extra push out in front of them to avoid backing up before kicking.

Partner Passing Competition

Skills
Accurate passing

Drill Description
Set up one square ten by ten yards for every four players. Inside each square place three cones with a disc cone on the top and three without. Each player is paired up with a partner who is on the opposite side of the square, with one ball between them. Two pairs are assigned to the same square, with only one player assigned to each side of a square, across from his partner. One pair is trying to knock over all of the cones with disc cones on top and one pair is trying to knock over the regular cones. The pair to succeed first is declared the winner for that round. You may play several rounds or switch pairs around so that they challenge another group.

Coaching Tips
To encourage side of the foot passing, you can make a rule that it only counts if you kick it properly. Many young players will continually kick with their toe and form bad habits if you don't constantly remind them how to kick properly.

Fun Soccer Drills that Teach Soccer Skills

Line Switch

Skills
Passing
Trapping
Throw-ins

Drill Description
Divide the group into two teams and line them up in two single file lines facing each other but about twenty feet apart. Give the ball to the person in front of one line and tell this player to pass the ball to the person in front of the other line. After passing the ball, the player who just kicked it runs to the back of the other line. On the way to the other line, give the team something crazy to do such as turn around five times, do three somersaults, jump over the cone, etc. Everyone will cycle through both lines back and forth while practicing the skill.

Variation
Have this set up as a competition between two groups and challenge them to make ten passes before the other team does.

Coaching Tips
The first few times doing this drill you might need to really remind players where to go next; you might, with cones or other markers, make a clear trail for the players to follow to the end of the other line.

Pass Around, Dribble Around

Skills
Trapping
Turning and dribbling
Passing

Drill Description
The group stands in a circle with a cone two yards behind each player.
One person starts with the ball and passes to someone who doesn't
have a ball. The person receiving the pass must trap it, turn and dribble
around the cone behind her before passing to someone else in the
circle who does not have a ball. Start this drill with one ball, then add a
few more as it gets moving.

Variation
Divide the group into pairs and give each pair one soccer ball. The
two players stand about ten yards apart and there's a cone behind each
player. One person passes to the other who traps the ball, turns and
runs around the cone behind her and then passes back.

Coaching Tips
Emphasize making eye contact with the person you are going to pass
to, to make sure this person is ready for the pass. Put as many balls
as you can into play without having so many that there aren't open
players to pass to. Emphasize gaining control of the ball by trapping
it or by lightly tapping it in the direction the player is going. Also
emphasize going to meet the ball that has been passed to you rather
than simply waiting for it to reach you.

Passing Drills

Ball Hit Ball

Skills
Accurate side of the foot pass

Drill Description
Divide the team into pairs and each pair should have two balls and one disc cone. Each pair spreads out about ten yards apart and places the disc cone in between them with one of the soccer balls sitting on top of the cone. The players take turns trying to kick the ball back and forth to knock the ball in the middle off of the cone. If the ball is knocked down the person who hit it gets to yell a cheer of excitement before placing the ball back on the cone. For added competition, ask each player at the end how many times they knocked the ball over. Or each pair can total up both of their scores for a team score.

Variations
If you do not have disc cones or extra soccer balls, simply place a cone between each pair that the players try to knock over.

Place one ball on a disc cone in the middle of a circle of players, but each person is across from his partner. Pairs kick back and forth and get one point each time one of them knocks the ball off of the cone. For this drill, to avoid a player getting hit with a ball when setting it back up, it is best if the coach sets the ball back on the cone after each knock over.

Coaching Tips
Emphasize proper side of the foot passing by only awarding a point when correct form is used.

One Touch Pass Contest

Skills
To pass the ball on the first touch
Passing with the inside of the foot

Drill Description
Divide the team into pairs with one ball between them and have them stand about five yards apart facing each other. When you say "go," each pair will pass back and forth and can only touch the ball once when kicking it back to her partner. The players should count out loud how many kicks they get or have a coach or parent count for each pair. If a ball stops at anytime, that team has to start their count over. After a time limit, ask each pair to announce the highest number of kicks they got between them without the ball stopping. Try this again and challenge each group to beat its old score.

Variation
If you have a small team you can have one pair "go" at a time while the others count out loud how many kicks they get.

Coaching Tips
Emphasize standing on balls of your feet and bouncing lightly to be ready to receive a quick pass and to return it quickly.

Soccer Bowling

Skills
Side of the foot passing

Drill Description
Set up as many "bowling lanes" as you have cones for or one for every two players. Use six cones for each lane and set them up in a bowling fashion with one in front, two behind that and then three behind this. Designate a starting point five to ten yards away, depending on the age and skill level of your team. Each player gets two turns to knock as many cones over as possible while another player is waiting to set up the cones, before the next turn. If they are in pairs, have them switch off or go to the end of the line after setting up the cones. To emphasize proper passing technique, the ball must be kicked using the side of the foot or the points do not count.

Variation
Work on long distance ground kicks by setting the starting point farther away from the cones.

Coaching Tips
By only being allowed to score when a side of the foot pass is used, it will force players to use this method of passing during the drill and hopefully, when done enough at practice, to transfer to game situations.

Passing Into the Square

Skills
Accurate passing
Controlling the weight of your pass

Drill Description
Using cones or disc cones set up four small squares two yards by two yards, each placed ten yards apart from the others, thus forming a large square with the small squares as the corners. Start in one square, and everyone has a ball and tries to kick it so that it rolls into the next square and comes to a stop inside the square. Everyone should kick to the same square but take turns. If a ball stops inside the square, the kicker gets a point. After everyone has kicked, go to the square the balls are in and the players kick to the next square from this spot. Continue around the square in this manner until one player gets four points and declare him the winner. If you have a large team, divide the group into smaller teams and set up several squares.

Variations
Set up a large circle of squares and divide the group into small teams of two to four players. Start the game with one team in every other square and have them move around the circle, kicking into the next square.

Set up one square for each player in a large square or rectangular shape with space between each square. When you say "go," everyone passes into the next square, moving in a clockwise direction. Each player is passing into a square that another player is already standing in. After each round, everyone goes to the square they were just aiming at and kicks their next ball from there. After taking a turn at each square, ask the players how many points they got.

Coaching Tips

This drill is good for players who blast the ball hard even when just passing to their own team or players who kick it too soft.

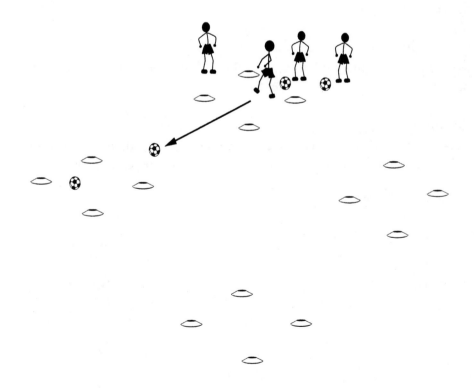

Pass it Back Relay

Skills
Dribbling and turning
Accurate Passing

Drill Description
Set up two lines about ten yards apart. Divide the group into two teams with one ball per team and put each team in a single file line on the same line. The first person in each line dribbles to the line that is ten yards away and turns (you may have a cone for them to turn around). After turning, they must pass back to the coach who is standing between the two teams (or, if you have an assistant coach, have one coach per team). After the ball is passed back, the player has to run back and tag the next person in line, who then receives the ball from the coach and goes next.

Variation
Rather than passing back to the coach, each player passes to the next person in line.

Coaching Tips
This is a good drill to encourage control and to provide the opportunity to look at each player individually and evaluate her passing skills.

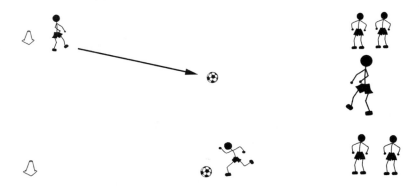

Fun Soccer Drills that Teach Soccer Skills

Back and Forth Passing Challenge

Skill
Passing and trapping while on the run

Drill Description
Set up six to eight cones in a line one yard apart. Each player has a partner and one ball between the two of them. One player is on one side of the cones and one on the other and they dribble down the field passing back and forth and trying to knock the cones over with each pass. Each team gets one point for every cone knocked over.

Variations
Set a time limit and challenge teams to knock over as many cones as possible within the time limit.

Instead of trying to knock the cones over, try to pass between the cones.

Coaching Tips
For larger groups it is a good idea to have more than one line going at a time with a coach or parent at each line to count cones knocked over and to help get set cones back up after each round. Encourage side of the foot passing and even trying to kick with the non-dominant foot when on that side, even though this is often very difficult for young players.

Soccer Kickball

Skills
Moving to the ball quickly
Passing
Kicking long distance

Drill Description
Set up three bases and home plate, or find an empty baseball field.
Divide the group into two teams, with one team starting at home plate
while the other team spreads out in the outfield. The coach is the
permanent pitcher and passes the ball to the person who is up (first to
kick). This person kicks the ball out into the outfield, as in kickball,
and then must run around all the bases and make it all the way to
home before the outfield team receives the ball, and everyone on their
team is passed to, and then the ball is passed back to the coach. If the
coach gets the ball before the kicker makes it back to home plate, then
the kicker is out. If the kicker makes it to home plate first, he scores
a point for his team. You may play to three outs and switch or have
everyone kick once and count how many home runs are made by each
team when everyone kicks once.

Coaching Tips
This is a good teamwork drill and encourages players to all be aware
of where the ball is and – if still needing to receive the ball – to call
out for a pass.

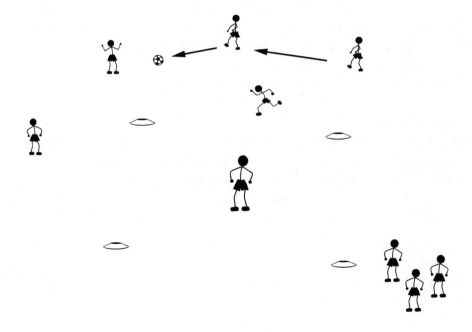

Pass Left or Right?

Skills
Dribbling
Passing
Receiving the pass
Making the best choice

Drill Description
This is a progression drill. The team lines up on the center line in the middle of the field while the coach is off to the side of the goal but out in the field a ways. Each player dribbles, one at a time from the center line, passes to the coach and then breaks for the goal to receive a pass and to take a shot on goal. After a few rounds of this, add another cone on the opposite side of the coach and have another coach (or player) stand by it. Add a defender who at first doesn't try hard to get the ball. One player at a time dribbles towards the defender who should go left or right forcing the pass to one of the two coaches who is on a cone. After passing, the player should run to the open space for the pass and then shoots on goal. The last stage of this drill is for the defender to try and get the ball and the shooter can choose to pass to either person on the cones or to dribble into the goal for a shot.

Coaching Tips
Prior to this drill I ask players to tell me when it is best to pass (when someone else is open and you are challenged) and when it is best to dribble (when not challenged and/or none of your teammates are open). I emphasize making the "best choice."

Find the Open Player

Skills
Communicating with each other
Finding the player who is ready to receive a pass
Passing
Trapping

Drill Description
Stand in a circle with one player in the middle. Three players in the circle start with a soccer ball. The Person in the middle of the circle must find someone who has a soccer ball and call her name for a pass. The person whose name is called then passes her ball to the person in the middle, who traps it and finds someone else who does not have a ball and passes it to her. After this, the person in the middle finds someone else who has a ball and asks for a pass. Continue in this manner and switch off players in the middle until everyone has a chance to participate.

Variation
For a large group, you may put two people in the middle or have two smaller groups going at the same time.

Coaching Tips
Emphasize looking at the person you are receiving the pass from and calling out their name. Also, the quicker the passes in this drill the better.

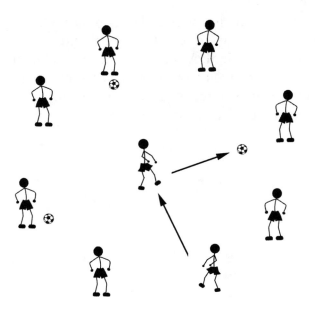

Player Pinball

Skills
Passing and trapping while moving down field
Shooting while on the run

Drill Description
Depending on the size of your team, place one or two cones on each side of the field between the goal and the center line in a zigzag manner. Place one player in front of each cone and the rest in a single file line with a ball at the center line. The players in line go one at a time passing to the first player on a cone, receiving a pass back then on to the next player, until passing to all the players on the cones and shooting on goal. When a player on a cone receives a ball, he should make a pinball noise when passing it back. To give everyone a chance to be a passer, switch off players on the cones.

Coaching Tips
Emphasize the "give and go" where players pass while moving and then the ball should be passed back to them, slightly in front of them so they can run onto the ball. Also, if players are looking up while dribbling, they can find their targets easier without stopping. This is a bit advanced for much younger children, but 'passing' while moving down field is good practice for future skills.

Fun Soccer Drills that Teach Soccer Skills

Find Your Friend

Skills
Receiving a pass and looking up to find a player before making a quick pass

Drill Description
Spread the team out into a large circle with one player in the middle. The coach, also a part of the circle, has all of the balls in a pile. The coach passes one ball at a time to the person in the middle and calls out the name of another player. The person in the middle must trap the ball, find the player whose name was called and quickly pass to that person. This person then traps the ball and dribbles it around the outside of the circle back to the coach and puts it in the ball pile before returning to her spot in the circle. The coach continues to make quick passes to the person in the middle. Switch off frequently to give everyone a chance to be in the middle.

Coaching Tips
Emphasize the benefits of moving quickly and of looking up as soon as a ball is received, so as to more easily find an open player or see if a defender is coming.

Cone Soccer

Skills
Accurate passing
Defending the goal

Drill Description
Give each player a cone and a soccer ball. Give the group a designated area they can place their cone in, and on the "go" signal everyone should place his cone somewhere within that area. Once everyone has found a spot, have each one put his cone on the ground. You can make up a story about why each player has to guard his cone and protect it, but also explain why he cannot touch it while guarding it. On the "go" signal, everyone tries to knock over everyone else's cone by kicking their soccer ball into it while at the same time guarding their own cone. Before the game starts, announce to the group what it is they have to do in order to return to the game (i.e. run a lap, dribble the soccer ball around a tree and back, etc.) after their cone is knocked over. Once someone has been eliminated they can return to the game, set up their cone and start playing again.

Variation
Each player has his own goal that he is guarding while, at the same time, trying to score on each of the other's goals. Award one point for each goal scored, but two points may not be scored on the same goal in a row.

Coaching Tips
This is one of those drills that is good for the coach to play to even out the number of times the more skilled player's cones are knocked over, so that the weaker players are not the first ones out all the time.

Run Coyote Run

Skills
Accurate kicking and speed when running

Drill Description
Select two players to be the kickers and give them all of the soccer balls. The rest of the team lines up on a line without a soccer ball (they are the runners). Set up a line opposite from where the runners are that they must run across. The kickers are on each side and try to kick their balls into the people who are running across when the kickers say, "Run Coyotes Run" (or whatever the name of your team is). Once a player is hit by a ball from the knee down they join either of the kickers and try to hit those who are running across. Each time the group makes it to the end line they should wait for the kickers to gather up the balls before running back to the other side. The last two players to make it across without being hit by a ball become the next kickers.

Variations
Players running across each dribble a ball and the kickers must hit the ball the opponent is dribbling to get her out. Start with more kickers on the side than just two for this.

The coach (or one of the kickers) decides how the players must move across the play area each time (hopping, skipping, walking, running backwards, etc.).

When a player gets hit she must mark (with a disc cone) the spot where she was hit, and then try to get others out by kicking from this spot.

Yell, "switch" in the middle of the game and runners have to reverse and make it back to the other line before you yell switch again.

Coaching Tips

The older the kids are, the more spread out the kickers should be from the field where the players are running through. This drill is better for younger players who do not have the ability to kick too hard yet.

Soccer Tag

Skills
Accuracy when kicking
Looking up when dribbling and speed when running

Drill Description
Mark off an area that the group must stay in during the game.
Designate two people to be "it" and give each a ball. These two
players dribble around and try to kick their ball into one of the players
without a ball in order to tag them. The players who are not "it" can
run anywhere in the area and try to not be hit by a ball. Once someone
is tagged with the ball, they must take that ball and dribble it around a
designated area and back to the game area where they become "it."

Variations
Play the same game but the two people who are "it" share one ball and
the person who kicked it switches with the person who got hit.

Have a pile of balls outside the playing area, and as soon as someone
gets hit he gets a ball and also become "it." Play until there is one
remaining player who then becomes "it" for the next round.

Coaching Tips
Sometimes younger players always want to be "it" but when they have
to run around a cone and back before their chance to become "it,"
there is more incentive for them to try harder to play the game fair.

Minefield in the Soccer Field

Skills
Accurate passing
Teamwork

Drill Description
Using disc cones, make a square about twenty yards by twenty yards. Spread out all of your regular cones inside the square. At the start of this drill, explain the story of the minefield. "If you go into the square you will become a superstar soccer player with special soccer powers, but the square is filled with mines and cannot be entered into until all the mines are dismantled. The only way to dismantle the mines is to knock them over with a soccer ball." Everyone should start with a soccer ball and tries to work as a team to get all of the cones knocked over. If a ball is kicked into the area and does not come back out it must stay inside the square and is lost. If all the balls are lost but all the cones are not knocked over, then the team can start over and see if they can knock more cones over the next time.

Coaching Tips
Of course you can change the story, but the drill is still the same. You might make it so they have to knock over a certain number of cones to be successful. Often, the first round players lose all of their balls fairly quickly, but after a few rounds they will figure out that they have to kick it hard enough to come back out of the square. Or, if a ball is reachable without touching the ground inside the square, they can help each other get the ball. And if there is just one ball left, it can be used to knock other balls out. A great teamwork drill!

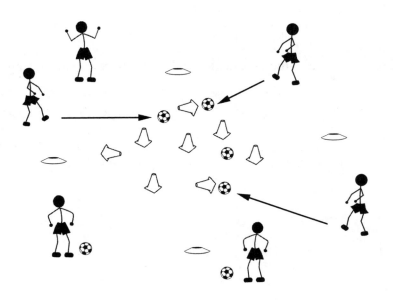

Cone in the Zone Knock Over

Skills
Accurate passing and shooting

Drill Description
Set up a lane using two rows of disc cones that are about fifteen yards wide and as long as you want to make the lane. In the middle of the lane, place several cones in a line that is spread out. Divide the group into two teams; and one team is on one side of the lane and the other team is across from them on the other side. Players can't cross the line into the lane, but try to knock the cones over by kicking their ball into them. If a cone gets knocked or a ball gets stuck in the lane the coach runs in and sets the cone up or kicks the ball out. Teams get one point for each cone knocked over and one point each time the coach is hit by a ball when inside the lane setting cones back up or kicking balls out.

Variation
Players take turns being the one setting up the cones and kicking the balls out while acting as a moving target.

Coaching Tips
For older teams, make the lane wider and move faster when setting up cones!

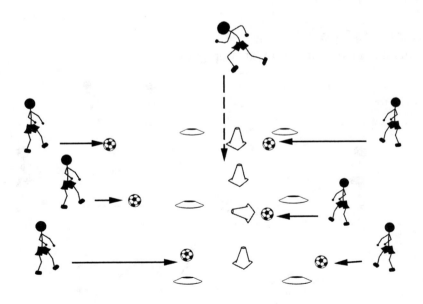

Kick Through

Skills
Passing accuracy

Drill Description
Set up two lines about ten yards apart and have players line up on either of these lines, facing each other with a ball. The coach and assistant have one ball between them and are lined up on the ends. The coaches pass back and forth while players try to hit the ball that was passed by kicking their ball into it. One point is awarded for each hit.

Variation
Divide the team into groups of four and set up a square with one player on each corner. One player does not have a ball and the person across from her passes the ball across the square while the other two players try to hit the ball with a pass. Allow each pair to have a number of turns before switching so the other two get a chance to try and hit the ball.

Coaching Tips
This can also be a good warm up game.

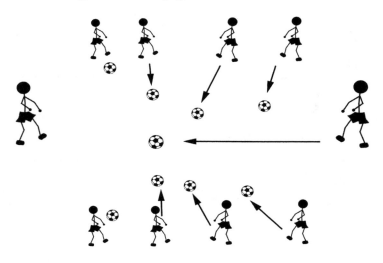

Goal line Soccer

Skills
Moving quickly to the ball and passing

Drill Description
Divide the group into two teams and have one team stand on one goal line and one team on the other. Call out a characteristic (i.e. everyone wearing red, with blue socks on, with long hair, etc.). Everyone who matches that characteristic runs out into the field and tries to score on the opposite side by kicking the ball across the end line. There may be more than one person on each team, and the teams may be uneven in number but that's OK. Those who are left on the end line turn into goalies and try to stop the ball from crossing the goal line (with or without using their hands). After a goal is scored or after a set amount of time, have the players return to their side and call out a new characteristic.

Coaching Tips
Encourage spreading out and passing, especially when one team outnumbers the other and has an advantage.

Mark Your Spot

Skills

Accurate kicking and quick running

Drill Description

Place one disc cone on each side of the field. Select two players to be
"it" first and have one stand by one cone and one by the other, each
with a pile of soccer balls. Everyone else starts on the end line. The
coach yells "go" and everyone runs across the field and tries to get to
the other end line without being hit by a ball that is kicked by one of
the kickers. If hit by the ball below the knee, they also become "it,"
only they mark a spot in the area where they got hit and only kick from
there during the next round with their own pile of balls. Once everyone
makes it to the other side, the coach yells "go" again until there are
two people left and they become the first two kickers for the next
game.

Coaching Tips

Have a pile of disc cones that you give to each player as they are hit
and let them know where the spot was that they were hit.

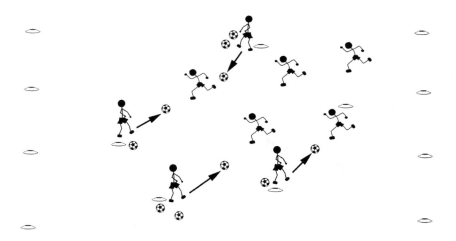

To the Other Side

Skills
Quick kicks

Drill Description
Divide the group into two teams, across from each other with a line of disc cones separating them. Everyone starts with a ball and when the coach says "go," each team tries to get all the balls to the other side. When the coach says "stop," the team with the least amount of balls on their side of the line is declared the winner.

Coaching Tips
This game can be played for any amount of time and is a good drill to get the kids moving or to simply fill a few minutes. This could also be used for a warm up drill.

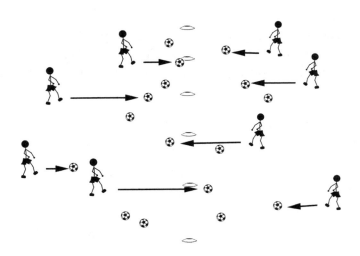

Island Ball

Skills
Accurate kicking and fast running

Drill Description
Create an "island" by making a circle with disc cones about two yards in diameter. Gather all the balls into a pile on the island and select one or two players to be "it" on the island. The rest of the team runs in a circle around the island (you can set up cones to mark boundaries they have to stay inside when running). The players on the island try to kick a ball into the runners (below the knees). If a player is hit she becomes a kicker as well and joins those on the island. Play until there are two players left who start the next game on the island.

Variations
Once a player gets hit they become a ball retriever and gather balls for those who are on the island.

Have the runners do different things when running around the island (hop, skip, walk, run backwards, etc.).

Coaching Tips
Any parents who are around can help retrieve stray balls to make this game easier for the kicker/s until there are lots of kickers and few runners and then it is good for the players to retrieve their own balls.

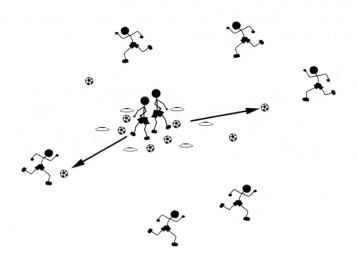

Outside the Square Cone Knock Over

Skills
Accurate passing
Taking control of a ball when opposition is near

Drill Description
Using disc cones make a square about twenty by twenty yards. Place one regular cone outside the square on each side about ten yards beyond the square and put all of the balls in the middle of the square. On the "go" signal everyone can run into the square and get a ball. Everyone tries to knock over any of the four cones by kicking a ball into them. If a ball goes out of the square anyone can go and get it but must bring it back into the square before kicking it at a cone. Anyone can take a ball from anyone else at anytime and use it to knock over a cone. Give "points" to anyone who knocks over a cone and play several rounds of this game but take away one ball prior to each round until there are just a few balls left.

Variation
Play this game in teams and you can't take the ball from your own team but can take it from people on the other team and give points to the whole team when someone knocks a cone over.

Coaching Tips
Encourage quick movement, shielding and heads up when dribbling to keep possession and to keep other players away from your ball. When a player doesn't have a ball he has to work at getting it by moving quickly and keeping his eye on the ball.

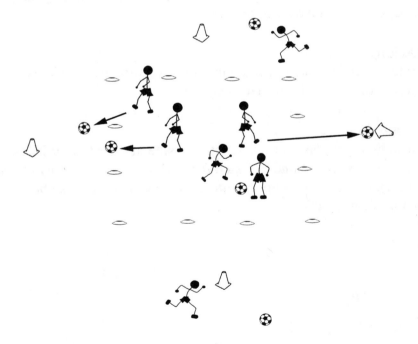

Ready, Aim, Fire

Skills
Accurate kicking

Drill Description
Use disc cones to mark off a circle about ten yards in diameter (or use the center circle of a soccer field) and place as many cones as you have in the middle. You can bunch the cones up or spread them out. Each player has a ball on the outside of the circle and when you yell "ready, aim, fire" everyone kicks her ball at the same time and tries to knock over as many cones as possible. Each player then quickly finds any ball and dribbles it to the outside of the circle where they set it up and wait for another "ready, aim, fire." Before starting this drill, ask the team how many rounds they think it will take to knock all of the cones down and challenge them to meet this goal. After all the cones are knocked over, set the cones up to do this again with a goal of getting all the cones knocked over in fewer rounds.

Variation
Count to ten after each shot and only those who are ready to kick when you yell "fire" can kick for that round.

Coaching Tips
If you want to get players to kick with the side of their foot or laces, this is a good type of game to watch for toe kicks and to set any cones back up that were knocked over with a toe kick. This can also be used as a great warm up drill.

Passing Alley

Skills
Passing accuracy

Drill Description
Set up cones in a line, using four or five cones for each line spread out, about ten yards long and about two yards apart. Divide the team into pairs. Each pair has one ball and is across from each other between two of the lines of cones (the "alley"). Players pass back and forth, keeping the ball in their own alley. If a ball hits a cone or goes into another alley the kicker must run around the entire group while his partner retrieves the ball and sets the cone back up.

Variations
Each pair gets one point for each successful pass they make down their alley.

For more skilled players, make the alleys closer together or have them kick a longer distance to each other.

Coaching Tips
This is a good drill for those players who constantly kick the ball wide to one side or the other. Watch their follow through when kicking to make sure they don't cross the kicking foot over the plant foot after making contact with the ball. This is a common reason young players kick to the side.

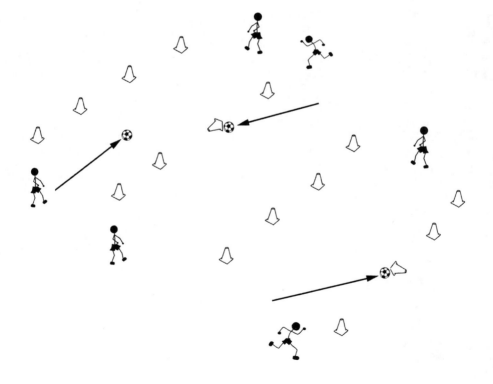

Long Kicks

At times during the game, long kicks will be taken so as to move the ball down the field on a corner kick, goal kick, or free kick. To gain more distance, you want these kicks to go up in the air. The drills in the chapter are fun games that require the ball to be kicked a longer distance.

When taking a long kick, the run to the ball should be at a slight angle and the non-kicking foot should be placed slightly behind the ball and to the side. The ball should be struck with the top of the foot on the under side of the ball. For power, the knee should snap forward. To make the ball go up into the air, the kicker should lean back after taking the kick.

Long Kick Drills

Characteristic Soccer Golf

Skills
Kicking towards a target

Drill Description
Select one player by stating a characteristic (i.e. a person with the most cleats on her shoe, with the longest hair, wearing the most red, etc.). The player who best fits the characteristic then gets to select a target somewhere in the practice area for the team members to aim at. Once a target is selected, everyone kicks her own ball toward the target and counts how many kicks it takes to get there. Once everyone reaches the target, select another characteristic to determine the next person who then picks out the next target. Continue in this manner by selecting a new characteristic each time. Make sure to look around the group and choose something that fits each person individually so that everyone gets one turn at selecting the target.

Variations
Play in pairs. Each player kicks her ball toward the target and then two partners select which ball ended up closest to the target, and they both kick their next ball from this spot. Continue in this manner to the target.

Play soccer golf by dribbling to each target rather than kicking, and the first one there gets a point. If a player kicks the ball too far out in front, then the coach can go after it and kick it in the other direction.

Coaching Tips
To keep this drill moving, have everyone kick at the same time toward the target. Most young players really don't know how many kicks it takes them to get to a target, so don't spend too much time deciding who got the least amount of kicks. Just ask "who got here in eight or less kicks" and they will all probably raise their hands.

Long Kick Drills

Partner Distance Kick Contest

Skill
Kicking a ball a long distance

Drill Description
You will need a large area for this drill. Divide the group into pairs and give each pair one ball and have the two players spread out and face each other. One player kicks the ball as far as he can toward his partner. His partner goes to the spot where the ball stopped and kicks the ball from there back towards his partner. The person who kicks the ball the farthest will eventually push his partner in that direction.

Variations
Allow the receiver to try and stop the ball and kick it from where it was stopped.

Do this drill in teams, taking turns kicking.

Coaching Tips
Younger players will almost always start out using the toe kick, which is difficult to direct and makes for bad habits later on. Even though you might not be successful at getting them to kick with their laces it is a good idea to constantly remind them about how to properly kick the ball.

Pair Goal Kick Challenge

Skills
Kicking the ball long distances to your teammate
Receiving a ball and turning
Dribbling towards the goal quickly

Drill Description
Set up a small cone field or play on a mini-size soccer field. This drill is done in pairs with one partner taking a kick from the goal box line (where a goal kick would be taken from) to the partner who is standing on the other goal box line. (Each pair is using the same line at the same time, but spread out along the line). As soon as the ball is kicked the partner of the kicker runs to meet the ball and turns and dribbles it back to the line where they then take a kick. To make this a game, challenge each pair to make as many kicks as possible in a given time; or challenge them to be the first group to take ten kicks.

Coaching Tips
Emphasize speed by challenging pairs to move quickly in order to "win" this drill. This challenge makes it more fun and more like a real game situation.

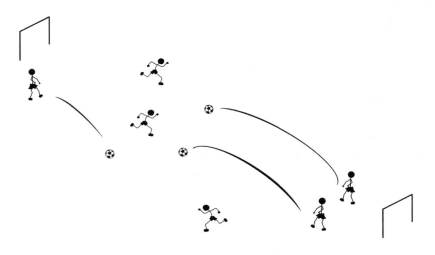

Up and Over

Skills
Kicking a ball a long distance in the air

Drill Description
Make a circle using disc cones that are ten to twenty yards in diameter.
Use the smaller size for younger kids but always make it challenging.
Inside the circle, place as many cones as you have scattered around.
Divide the team into pairs with each person across the circle from
her partner with one ball between them. The player with the ball tries
to kick it up over the circle to her partner without it touching the
ground inside the circle or without knocking over a cone. If a player
successfully kicks a ball over the circle then she gets to tell the whole
team something they have to do five times (jumping jacks, sit ups,
twirls, etc.). If a player hits a cone and knocks it over, this player has
to do five jumping jacks (or whatever you specify at the beginning of
the game). If no cones are hit or the ball hits the ground in the circle,
nothing happens and the other partner gets a turn.

Variations
If the kick goes up and over the circle, the kicker gets to yell a cheer
and jump up in the air with excitement instead of making the others do
an exercise.

Instead of trying to kick it over the cones, each player tries to hit the
cones when kicking to her partner and gets one point for each cone
that is knocked over.

Coaching Tips
I often have this drill set up when the players start showing up for
practice and pair them up as they arrive; this way it is easy to give each
player individual attention when assessing their kicking skills. If you
have players with more skill than the others, set up cones for them to
kick from that are farther away from the circle for an added challenge.

Long Kick Drills

In and Out

Skills
Kicking long balls
Trapping

Drill Description
Set up two equal sized squares using cones that are large enough for half the team members to move freely around in and kick balls out of. The squares should be at least ten yards apart (longer distances for older teams). Everyone should start with a ball. Players try to kick a ball through the other team's square. If any ball goes in and then goes out of any side of the other team's square, the team who kicked it gets one point. This includes balls that bounce off of players. If a ball is stopped inside the square then a point is prevented and the team may kick it back. Any balls that are not stopped in the square can be retrieved by the nearest team and taken back to the team's own square to be kicked.

Coaching Tips
This is a good drill to encourage trapping and stopping the ball. It is helpful to have a coach or parent counting the points for each team.

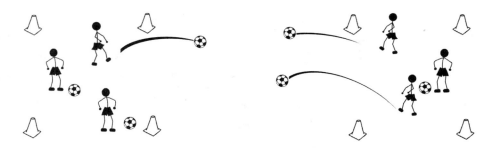

Hot Potato Ball

Skills
Quick movement

Drill Description
Set up a circle of cones or use the center circle of a regulation size
soccer field. Select one or two players to stand in the middle of the
circle while everyone else stands around the outside with the soccer
balls. On the "go" signal, everyone on the outside of the circle kicks
his ball into the circle. Those in the middle kick all of the balls out
and must stay in the middle until there is a moment when there are no
balls in the circle. Once a ball is kicked out, it can be kicked back in by
anyone.

Coaching Tips
A fun high paced drill that most players really like. If the players in the
middle kick the balls far out it is easier for them to win the game.

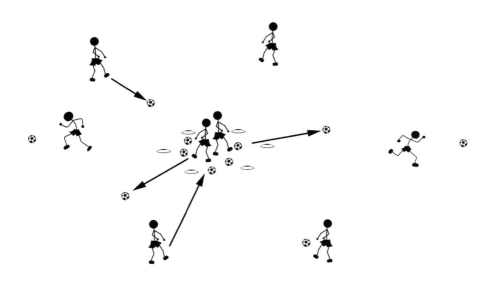

Red Rover, Red Rover, Kick your Ball Right Over

Skills
Defending a kick
Accurate ground kicks

Drill Description
Divide the group into two teams and line them up facing each other about ten yards apart. Give one team a ball and ask the other team to pick a player from the team with the ball. Once a person is selected, the whole team chants, "Red Rover, Red Rover, (name of person) kick your ball right over." The person whose name was called then kicks his ball on the ground toward the other team and tries to get it to go through their line. If the ball goes through the line, the kicker gets to take one person from the other team to his side; if the ball is blocked, then the kicker has to join the other team. Continue in this manner back and forth between the teams.

Variation
The player who has been called tries to dribble through the line rather than kick the ball.

Coaching Tips
After the team has been doing lots of running, this is a fun drill that involves everyone but still gives the players a bit of a break.

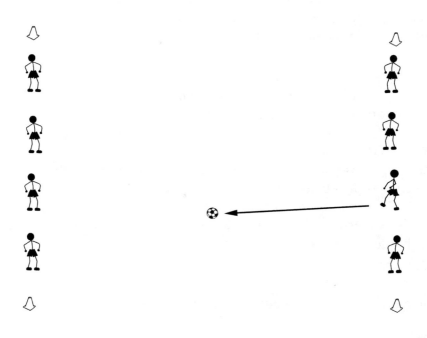

Long Kick Drills

Cone Knock Over

Skills
Accurate kicking
Blocking kicks

Drill Description
Divide the group into two teams with a line in between the two teams. Everyone starts with a ball on her own side and cannot go into the other side. Place the same number of cones (about five) on each team's side in a line that is spread out and the same distance from the center line (at least ten yards back). Place a line of disc cones in front of the target cones that make up the "cone zone." On the "go" signal, each team tries to kick the balls into the other team's cones to knock them over. Players cannot enter into the cone zone on their own side when guarding the cones unless they are retrieving a dead ball. Once a cone is knocked over, whoever hit it runs to the other side and picks up the cone and brings it back to her side to add to her team's cones. Once a team has all of the cones it is declared the winner, but this doesn't happen very often unless you play for a long time!

Variations
Leave cones that are knocked over down. The first team to get all of the cones on the other side down is the winner.

Set up a zone in between the two teams that both teams can dribble into to get closer to the cones they are trying to hit. Inside the zone, players can steal balls from each other.

Use other objects to knock over such as soda pop cans or empty two liter bottles.

Coaching Tips
Since each team is constantly loosing and gaining cones, this is a great

game that can be played for any length of time because it usually does not end before it is time to move on to something else. If possible, it is great to end the game when both teams have the same amount of cones and declare the game a "tie."

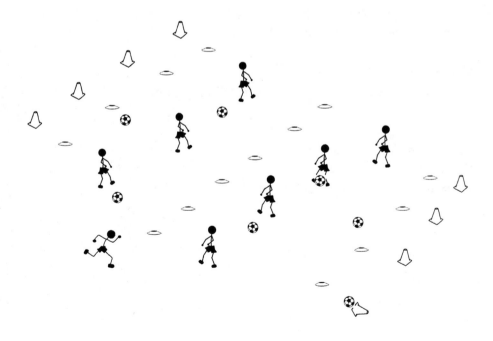

Soccer Spud

Skills
Gaining control of a high ball
Accurate kicking
Quick running

Drill Description
Everyone gathers around the coach who is holding a soccer ball. The coach throws the ball straight up into the air and calls out the name of one of the players. The person whose name is called races to the ball and brings it under control (no hands of course), while everyone else scatters in all directions as fast as they can. As soon as the chosen player has the ball she yells "Spud" and everyone else must freeze in place. The player with the ball kicks it toward one of the frozen players in attempt to hit them with the ball. A frozen player cannot move her feet but can move the rest of her body. If the person is hit she gets a letter (SPU or D) to spell spud. If nobody is hit by the ball then the kicker gets a letter. Whoever gets a letter gets to throw the ball into the air and call out a name for the next round.

Variation
Give everyone a number and instead of calling out names call out a number.

Coaching Tips
Keep this drill moving by telling everyone to gather quickly around the new thrower before each round.

Long Kick Drills

The Big Kick Contest

Skills
Long kicks
Throw-ins
Goalie punts and throws

Drill Description
Everyone starts on a designated line with a ball, facing the coach who is standing facing the line. The coach asks the team how far they can kick by walking backwards and saying "can you kick this far?" When the team tells the coach to stop at the point where they think they can kick, he calls out their names one at a time to put it to the test.. After everyone has kicked, they gather up the balls and go back to the line; then the coach moves forward or backwards to give them a new distance to kick to based on how close they were on the first try. Continue in this manner until everyone makes it to the coach before changing to throw-ins, punts, or goalie throws.

Variations
Have everyone kick at the same time.

Simply hold a contest to challenge the children to kick it farther than anyone else.

Coaching Tips
This is a good drill for looking at each player individually and giving pointers when he is practicing a skill.

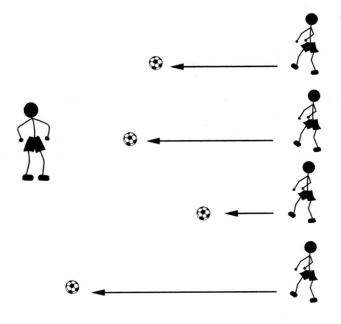

Long Kick Drills

Goal Kick - Pass

Skills
Getting open for a goal kick
Receiving a pass and then passing it up field to an open player

Drill Description
Place a pile of balls near the area where a goal kick should be taken.
One player starts out as the kicker and one player starts out as a runner
and everyone else is lined up waiting to be the next kicker. The first
runner runs to a cone set up out in the field and as soon as she gets to
the cone the kicker kicks the ball to her. She receives the ball and turns
toward the other goal at the other end of the field, where a coach is
open and ready for a pass. The player then kicks the ball to the coach
and then breaks for the goal. The coach passes the ball back to the
player in front of the goal where she takes a shot on goal. If you have
a skilled player you can replace the coach with this player after a few
rounds. The player who was the kicker then becomes the runner for the
next kicker. You can have this drill running to the left and right sides of
the field at the same time.

Coaching Tips
This drill is great for getting players to focus on taking goal kicks to
the side of the field and not up the middle, and for teaching where
the best spot to get open is. Many young players will stand about two
yards away from the kicker in a big group, hoping to get the ball in a
game.

Corner Kick Challenge

Skills
Taking accurate corner kicks

Drill Description
Set up two cones in front of each goal that represents where teammates should stand when a corner kick is taken. Divide the team into four groups (two groups if you only have use of one goal or a small area to practice in). Each group is on one corner and the players take turns with their teammates taking a corner kick and trying to hit a cone. Give one point to each team that hits a cone.

Coaching Tips
Young players often kick corner kicks behind the goal and have trouble taking a good corner kick that is in front of the goal. This is a good drill to encourage kicking balls in front of the goal.

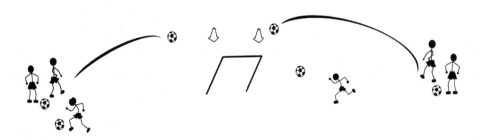

Defense and Dribbling With Pressure

In this chapter there are several drills where a defender is introduced so as to place pressure on a player who is dribbling. As well as emphasizing dribbling skills, these drills can be used to focus on defensive and tackling skills.

When teaching defending skills to young players, the main points are: keep your eye on the ball when going in for a tackle, keep yourself between the ball and the target, and, when beat by an opponent, cut him off by moving quickly to get between the ball and the goal. Many young players will simply chase behind an opponent and are rarely able to catch the opponent. Instead, the chaser should move to get between the other player and the goal. It's easy to teach young players that the closest person goes to the ball and that everyone else should be marking other players or backing up the defender in case they get beat. This helps prevent a huge crowd from going after the ball, while leaving the other team open.

Often, with the younger age groups, the most fearless player is the best defender because the dribbling skills of the opponent do not require much more than running up and taking the ball away. However, proper tackling skills can be taught so that young players can begin to learn skills needed in the future when dribbling and passing skills are acquired by the opponent.

When approaching an opponent who is dribbling, the first thing a player should do is move quickly, running with "big steps" toward the player in possession of the ball. When closing in on the opponent, "small steps" should be used to slow down and to keep proper distance from the dribbler. The defender should be close enough to threaten the offensive player with the ball but far enough away to assure that the dribbler cannot dribble around the defender easily. If a defender moves in too fast and swipes at the ball, a skilled dribbler can easily tap the ball to the side and move quickly around the defense. The defender should have the defensive stance of crouching with knees slightly bent so he can easily move in all directions. One foot should be in front of the other so that the defender can kick at a stray ball when the dribbler makes a mistake, and thus direct the player with the ball in the direction the defender wants this player to go. Teaching this type of advanced defensive skills to children isn't easy, but some of them may be able to grasp this concept at an early age.

Defense and Dribbling with Pressure Drills

Chase

Skills
Speed while dribbling
Shielding the ball from a defender
Taking the ball away from someone running with the ball when you
are the defender

Drill Description
Everyone starts out with a ball except for one person who is "it." Give
the group a destination some distance away that they must dribble to
and back from. Those with a ball must dribble as fast as they can while
the "it" person tries to take anyone's ball away. Once a person has her
ball taken away then she becomes "it" and tries to take someone else's
ball away. (She cannot take the ball away from the person who took it
away from her.) The play continues this way until everyone returns to
the start line.

Variations
Dribble to several different locations and designate a different person
to be "it" once you reach each destination.

For larger groups start out with two or three people who don't have a
ball.

Set up a large square and put a pile of balls in the middle. There should
be one less ball than there are players. On the "go" signal everyone
runs to get a ball. The one person who does not get a ball must steal
one or chase someone out of the square to get that individual's ball. At
the end of a time limit, the person who does not have a ball must do
something funny, such as perform a dance or sing a song for the group
(or whatever consequence you decide upon).

Coaching Tips

As a coach you might allow the last person to take away your ball; that way you are the only one at game's end without a ball.

Dribble to the number

Skills
Dribbling to a target
Stopping a ball
Shielding and defending

Drill Description
Put the numbers one through six on six different cones spread out in a large circle. These numbers do not have to be in order around the circle. Once the cones are set up, select one player to stand in the middle of the circle, without a ball, while the rest of the team stands around the circle, each with a ball. The person in the middle calls out one of the numbers and everyone tries to dribble to that cone and stop his ball at the cone, without the person in the middle getting the player's ball. If a player's ball is kicked away by the person in the middle, then that player joins the first person as a defender in the middle . Once everyone makes it to the designated cone, or turns into a defender, the person calls out another number. Play until there is one person left; then that person starts the next game.

Variations
Put the numbers one, two, and three on each of the two cones and place them around. When a number is called, players have to choose which of the two cones with that number they would like to go to.

If you don't have cones with numbers on them simply place one cone in one spot, two in another, three in another, and so on.

Coaching Tips
Emphasize keeping control of the ball when dribbling. Younger players often kick the ball out too far ahead of themselves when dribbling and it is then easily taken away by a defender.

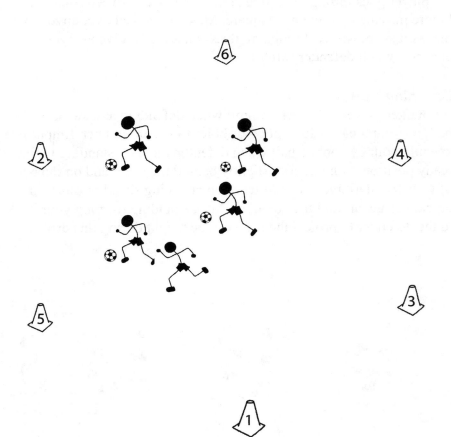

Gauntlet

Skills
Defending and dribbling

Drill Description
Set up three squares in a line about ten yards by ten yards with five yards of space between each square. Select one player to stand in each of the three squares. One player at a time tries to dribble through all three squares without getting her ball kicked out or taken away from her. After making it (or getting one's ball kicked out of the first square) the player goes through to a free zone (the place between squares) before moving onto the next square. Make a big deal over anyone who makes it successfully through all three squares. To give everyone a chance, switch defenders after a while.

Coaching Tips
A younger player will over-commit when defending and swipe at the ball, making it easier for a good dribbler to get around her. Emphasize keeping your eye on the ball when defending and on standing in the ready position with one foot slightly behind the other and on the balls of your feet. Dribblers should work on changing speed or direction quickly to get around the defender. Also, shielding (turning your back to the defender to protect the ball) can be taught during this drill.

Ball Shield

Skills
Keeping the ball close when dribbling and shielding from a defender

Drill Description
Mark off a large area with four cones and divide the group into pairs. One person in each pair starts with the ball and the other person is the defender. Demonstrate how to shield the ball with your body when dribbling by keeping your body between your ball and the defender. Count to ten and challenge the players with the balls to keep possession of their ball for the entire ten seconds; then switch so that the other players has a chance. After this you may add time and challenge the players with balls to keep possession for fifteen seconds.

Coaching Tips
To give everyone a chance to practice against different opponents, have the players switch partners after a few rounds.

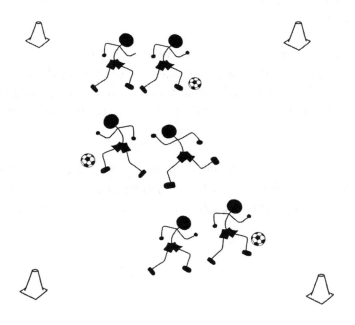

Defender in the Middle

Skills
Dribbling and Defending

Drill Description
Select one person to be "it" who starts in the middle without a ball. Everyone else lines up on one line with a ball. When the person in the middle says "go" everyone dribbles across the field to the other side to a designated line. Once they cross the opposite line they are safe, but until they cross the line the person in the middle tries to get anyone's ball. If your ball is taken or kicked out by the person in the middle then you, too, become "it," and the next time the person in the middle says "go" you join in trying to get the ball away from those who are coming across.

Variations
Whoever's ball is taken must surrender his ball over to the person who was "it"; then this person is the new "it" until he gets the ball from someone else.

Two players are "it" and they have a ball while the rest of the players do not. As players try to run from one side to another the players in the middle try to kick their ball into any of the players to make them "it" as well (have a ready pile of balls on the side for the newcomers).

Coaching Tips
This is a fun drill to give players a good workout and to practice defending and dribble fake out moves such as change of speed, change of direction, and pulling the ball back in the other direction.

Defender Chase

Skills
Dribbling quickly while keeping control of the ball
Proper defending of a breakaway

Drill Description
Set the team up in two single file lines next to each other on the center line of the field and facing the goal. The players in one line have a ball. Tell the person in front of that line to "go" and she dribbles as fast as possible to the goal with the ball. Give this person a couple of seconds head start before sending the first person from the other line to act as a chasing defender. The person with the ball should not be allowed to shoot until getting into the goal box (or making a designated line). Have each player go to the end of the opposite line she came from when finished.

Coaching Tips
The defender should race to the open goal, not merely chasing the person with the ball but keeping the ball in sight. If a defender can get between the goal and the ball, they have a chance to stop the breakaway but often young players will chase the ball. To keep this drill moving quickly, send the next group before the first one is done.

Fun Soccer Drills that Teach Soccer Skills

Backwards Run

Skills
Keeping your eye on the ball when running to defend the goal

Drill Description
The players line up on the center line, facing the coach who has a ball. The coach dribbles toward the players while moving back and forth across the field. The players must run backwards so they can keep their eyes on the coach. Anytime the coach stops the ball all players must sit down as fast as possible, the last one standing gets a point. At the end of the activity, the player with the most points has to do a task or exercise assigned by the coach.

Coaching Tips
Many young players will immediately run toward to goal when the other team gets the ball and, because they are focused on the goal, miss an opportunity to take the ball away. Or a shot is taken when the player has his back turned. Teaching young players to always know where the ball is can be a valuable lesson.

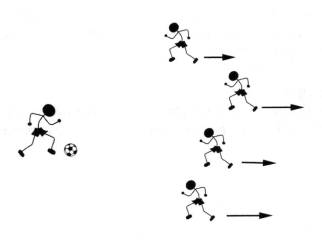

Shield from the Monster

Skill
Shielding your ball from a defender

Drill Description
Everyone starts with a ball inside an area that is about ten yards by
ten yards. Select one player to be "the monster." This player does
not have a ball and tries to kick everyone else's ball out of the area.
Once a player's ball is kicked out, she retrieves the ball and waits till
everyone's ball is kicked out. The last player to have her ball kicked
out is the "monster" for the next round.

Variations
Have kids do 10 jumping jacks before coming back in (or any other
task) and after a certain amount of time switch "the monster." Or,
if the monster gets everyone out at the same time she wins and can
switch with someone.

Everyone has a ball and tries to kick everyone else's ball out while
shielding her own ball, and then does a task before returning to
the game. A player wins if she is the only one in the middle when
everyone else is doing an exercise. Or, a player gets one point for each
ball she kicks out or forces out of bounds, and at the end the player
with the most points wins.

Coaching Tips
Prior to the drill it is helpful to show the players how to shield a ball
when dribbling, by keeping one's body between the opponent and the
ball.

Partner Keep Away

Skills
Passing and receiving the ball while moving down field
Defending

Drill Description
Divide the group into pairs and select one pair to start in the middle of the field as defenders. The other players line up with their partner on one end line. The first pair dribbles and passes back and forth down the field and tries to make it to the far line without getting their ball taken away. If they make it, they return to the back of the line for another try down the field. If their ball is taken away, they become the team in the middle who tries to take the ball away from the next two.

Coaching Tips
If the pair has to dribble a long ways to get to the defenders, then another pair can be started when the first group gets to the defenders. After a pair is on their way back to line, they have a longer way to go and it keeps everyone moving. Encourage pairs to stay spread out when coming down field and for the person with the ball to pass when challenged and/or when his partner is open.

Fun Soccer Drills that Teach Soccer Skills

Rock Paper Scissors and Score

Skills
Quick Dribbling
Quickly getting back to defend the goal

Drill Description
Divide the group into two teams and set up a small field with all the balls in a line in the middle of the field. Each team should have a coach or parent to help them decide if they want to be Rock, Paper or Scissors for the popular game. Once the teams secretly decide, they line up in the middle facing each other with the balls between them. The coach says "one-two-three" and, on three, everyone gives the signal for Rock, Paper or Scissors that their team decided on. The team that shows the winning hand wins and all the players on that team take a ball and dribble toward the opposite goal to try and score while the other team runs to defend. Defensive players cannot take a ball away until the shooters get past a certain line that you should set up in advance. The shooters get one point for each goal scored by the time you count to twenty. Set the balls up in the middle and do it again!

Coaching Tips
You will most likely have to shout out who the winning team is after they show their hand because younger players can't remember quickly if rock beats paper or what beats what.

Capture the Ball

Skills
Dribbling with speed
Dribbling against a defender

Drill Description
Using disc cones, set up a line across the field and divide the team into two even groups with one team on one side of the line and one on the other. On each side, make a box out of cones that is at least five yards behind the center line. Place three balls inside each box. Players try to go across the line and get the balls back to their own side without getting the ball taken away from them before they cross the line. Once a player runs across the line she can get tagged before getting to the box and sent back to her own side; if she makes it to the box she is safe till she leaves the box. Defenders may not enter into the box on their own side. When a player is dribbling out of the box the defenders may take the ball away and then the ball goes back into the box and the player must return to her side before trying again. Any ball that is successfully dribbled across the line is added to the box on that team's side. The first team to get all six balls is declared the winner.

Coaching Tips
This can be one of those never ending games since the balls can go back and forth. I like to call the game to an end and declare it a tie when both teams have three balls again.

Defense and Dribbling Drills

Team Play

When all the players on the field are in a big group chasing after the ball this is often referred to as "bunch ball," and it is not uncommon to see this with younger players. If you can teach a young player the concept of moving into the open space then you will have done an amazing job as a coach. Team play occurs when passing opportunities are created and when players work together to move the ball down the field.

When a player's teammate has the ball, the player should continually move into an open space so that she can be available for a pass or to draw a defender away from one's own teammates. The drills in this chapter focus on moving into the open space when a player does not have the ball and when her teammate does. The open space is that area on the field where there are no defenders between the player and her teammate who has the ball.

Team Play Drills

Circle Soccer

Skills
Spreading out
Moving to the open space
Accurate passing

Drill Description
Use disc cones to create small circles and place them around the
playing area. Make sure there are two or three more circles than there
are players. Each player stands in a different circle and one player
has a ball. The person with the ball must pass at the count of three
and can only pass to someone standing in a circle. A person can move
to an empty circle at any time, but only one person can be in a circle
at a given time. Once the player passes the ball, he must move to a
different circle. Once the team gets good at passing and moving, add
a defender who can go for the ball, after the count of three. Once the
team is quick enough, allow the defender to go for the ball at any time.

Coaching Tips
Encourage players to pass the ball quickly and encourage those players
who don't have the ball to call for it when in a good position to receive
the pass.

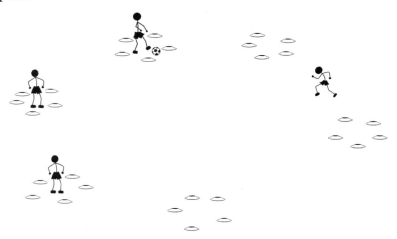

Partner Get Open

Skills
Passing to someone who is open
Moving to the open space

Drill Description
Use an existing line on the field or set up cones in a line. Divide the group into pairs and have one person from each pair stand on each side of the line, facing each other. Give one person from each pair a ball and challenge each pair to pass the ball across the line to one's partner as many times as possible in one minute, while at the same time preventing the other pairs from doing the same. After one minute, give the entire group just one ball, after which everyone still tries to pass the ball to her partner. You might make a rule that if a player has the ball on the kicking side it can't be taken away but the other side may defend against the partner who will be receiving the ball. This drill works best with four to six players; if you have more than this you may want to set it up in two different locations.

Coaching Tips
Encourage moving around and changing speed when trying to get rid of defenders and trying to get open for a pass from your partner.

Get to the Open Space!

Skills
Finding the open space on the field and moving to it

Drill Description
Prior to this drill, briefly explain to the players the benefits of moving to the open space during a soccer game. Set up four cones creating a large square and have all the players start inside the square. When the coach says "go," the players must run around the area until the coach yells "freeze." The coach then selects the player located in the largest space with no other players nearby. This player gets "one point." Play several rounds. You may want to add soccer balls after a few rounds so that players can practice moving into an open space while dribbling a soccer ball.

Coaching Tips
Younger players always clump around the ball in a game; so the more drills you do during practice to reward moving into the open space, the better.

Safety Square

Skills
Finding the open space with or without the ball

Drill Description
Using four cones, make a square that is about ten feet by ten feet in front of the goal and by the edge of the penalty box. The coach stands in the square and is safe from any defender. Start with one defender in front of the goal and line up the team in a single file line at the center line. One player at a time dribbles down the field toward the goal and, if being challenged by the defender, can pass to the coach at any time. The coach then is safe from a defender while in the square and passes back to the player when she gets open. After one round have the players become the player in the "magic square" and switch off the defender.

Coaching Tips
When dribbling toward the goal, players should decide who is more open; themselves or the person in the square. After passing, the player needs to quickly move around the field to find the open space in order to receive a pass. This is a good drill for helping them find the open space by pointing it out while in the square with the ball.

Target Goals

Skills
Spreading out
Passing
Getting Open
Defending

Drill Description
Set up two different cone types by placing a disk cone on top of half the cones or have two different colored cones, etc. Place three or four of each kind of cone around the soccer field. Divide the group into two teams and assign each team one of the two types of cones that they will try to knock over by kicking the ball into it. On the "go" signal, each team tries to knock over its own cones by kicking the ball into the cone. With both teams competing, there is only one ball. Emphasize spreading out, and kids should find open cones and run to these cones and call for a pass.

Variation
Instead of trying to knock cones over, set up several small goals – half with disc cones on them and half without; each team tries to score on one type of goal but can't score two consecutive goals on the same goal. Or, set up several goals and any team can score on any goal.

Coaching Tips
This is one of the best drills for encouraging players to get open. It works great when one coach or parent plays on each team to help spread the team out and to demonstrate getting open near a cone and passing to the open player. As a coach I will hold onto the ball and dribble around until a player on my team becomes open for a pass. This is also a great game for getting into shape since there is constant running and kids really seem to enjoy the competition.

Zone Soccer

Skills
Staying spread out and not crowding each other when playing
Moving to the open space
Passing to the open space.

Drill Description
On a soccer field create three zones with cones that divide the field lengthwise into three sections. Players come down the field in groups of three with one person in each zone. Give the group a set number of passes they have to make before they can shoot on goal. The players should go to the end of a different line after each shot on goal. After a few rounds, tell them that they can only pass and that no dribbling is allowed; after this, add a defender.

Variation
Divide the group into two teams and play a regular game of soccer; however, players are assigned a zone that they have to stay in during the game. Each player can only defend against a player who has the ball in his own area and has to pass if he wants to move the ball to another area.

Coaching Tips
This is a good drill for teams that have trouble staying away from each other during the game and who are always bunched up and need to work on separating. Play a regular scrimmage after this drill to help a team take this concept into a game situation.

Alligator Swamp

Skills
Moving off the ball into the open space for a pass
Finding the open person for a pass

Drill Description
For this drill take cones and turn them on their side and with a dry erase pen draw an alligator face on each one (or just keep it plain and call it an alligator). If you have disc cones, draw a turtle on each one.

This drill is a progression drill with several activities and can take a whole practice. Start by making the "Alligator Swamp," using the turtle cones as the edge of the swamp and placing the alligator cones on their sides around the inside of the swamp. The area should be about ten yards from one side to the other and whatever length you need to fit groups of two all along the swamp.

Divide the group into pairs. Explain to the group that nobody can go into the swamp unless they receive a ball after running through the swamp. If an alligator gets your ball (the ball touches a cone) he will eat it and you can only get it back if you do ten jumping jacks (or some other easy exercise). After this, do the following progression of drills with the swamp set up:

1. Both partners start on one side of the swamp, one partner has the ball and the other partner runs through the swamp to the other side for a pass; once the runner makes it through the swamp, her partner passes the ball. Do this several times, giving each person a chance to be both the runner and passer.
2. Use one coach or parent for each pair, the coach passes the ball to the pair and the first one to get the ball becomes the passer and the other one becomes the runner.
3. In a group of three players, one person starts with the ball and the other two run across. To pass the ball, the passer first selects the most open player or the player who seems most ready for a

pass.

4. In a group of three with a coach for each group, the coach passes the ball to the group and the first one to get it becomes the kicker and the other two run across for a pass.

5. With a group of three, do the same as above; but add a defender (you can take away the alligator cones at this point), then add two defenders, and then three.

Coaching Tips

This drill worked wonders for my five and six year old team. They started to run out for a pass as soon as one of their teammates got the ball instead of running as a bunch! Make sure to test your dry erase markers on your cones before drawing on all of them, to be sure they will wipe clean. Or, you can simply use the cones and call them alligators without drawing on them.

Magic Boxes

Skills
Passing the ball up field to an open player

Drill Description
Make a small field with the center line clearly defined by cones or discs. In front of each goal about five yards out, use cones to make a square big enough for a player to move around when trying to get open in front of the goal. Divide the group into two teams with one team on each side of the line. Select one player from each team to go to the "magic box" on the other side of the field from where their own team is. For this game the players on each team cannot cross the center line but can pass any ball that comes to their side to their player in the "magic box" who then tries to score. Players who do not have a ball try to prevent the player in the box on their side from getting a ball and scoring without going into the box. Start with three balls and then add balls or take them away depending on the flow of the game. Switch off players who are in the "magic box" so everyone gets a turn.

Variation
Add an additional magic box on each side so that players can dribble to and then pass to the person in the magic box in front of the goal, before returning to their side. Only one player can dribble into a box at a time.

Coaching Tips
After your team gets the concept of passing to someone who is in the magic box in front of the goal emphasize passing to this area in the game and for players to try to get open in front of the goal in the 'box'.

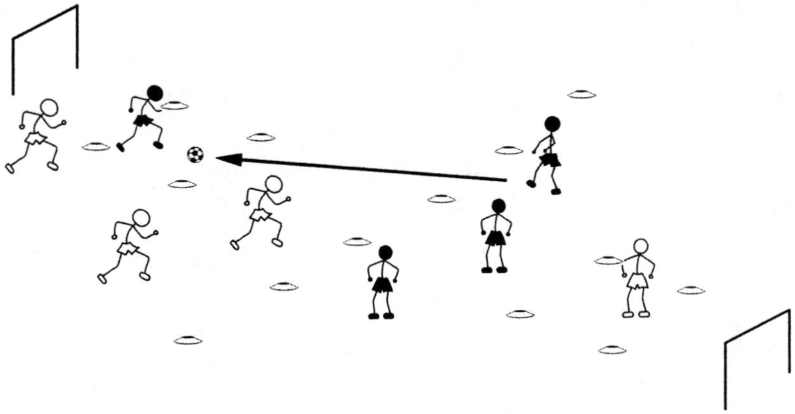

Magic Boxes - Two on Two

Skills
Spreading out
Passing to an open teammate

Drill Description
Divide the team into groups of four. For every four players, set up
two "magic boxes" that are about one yard by one yard and set these
two boxes about fifteen yards apart. Divide each group into pairs for
two on two competitions. Each pair tries to score on their opponent
by passing to each other from outside the box to inside the box that is
their designated goal to score on. When a player receives a pass inside
their box he must stop it for it to count as a score. Defending players
may not enter into the box. After a goal is scored, the defending team
gets to dribble the ball into play from the box.

Variation
As players master two on two, change the game to three on three.

Coaching Tips
Young players often bunch around the ball. The concept of passing or
being open is difficult to teach in large game settings, but by starting
with smaller examples of spreading out and teamwork the players can
learn the concept.

Whistle Stop Scrimmage

Skills
Spreading out and not bunching around the ball

Drill Description
Set up a small field and play a soccer game with three to five players on each team. (If you have more players, set up two fields or have a drill going on for one team while two teams play.) At any time during the game, blow a whistle and everyone must freeze where they are. The team with the most players bunched together has to do a task, or simple exercise as assigned by the coach. After the task is complete, ask players to spread out and move to the open space on the field before starting the game again.

Coaching Tips
This drill is very helpful for teams who tend to bunch around the ball all the time during a game (which is the case for many younger teams).

Playing for Points

Skills
Getting open
Passing down field
Breakaway
Defending

Drill Description
Divide the group into teams of three or four and play small sided games but for each game give out points for the following…
2 points if you pass to someone who can score
2 points if you are open for a pass near the goal
1 point if you score
1 point if you stop a breakaway
1 point if you have a breakaway and shoot before the other team gets to you
1 point if you stop a goal
If there are enough coaches (or parents) available, assign one to each team and give them a clipboard with the above list of points on the side and room for the player's names on the top. Each coach should watch her team (or both teams if there aren't enough coaches) and write down points during the game. After the scrimmage announce points and emphasize what each player did correctly. For added fun offer a small prize (candy, stickers, etc) for each point made or for each player who made at least five points.

Coaching Tips
This drill worked wonders for my girls team to get them to focus on spreading out and being in position for a pass. Of course there are always a few players who need to be given a few points for even attempting to accomplish any of the things on the list, even if they were not successful.

Eliminate and Support

Skills
Dribbling
Shielding
Passing
Getting to the open space

Drill Description
Divide the group into two teams and give one team a color jersey to wear to distinguish them from the other team. Each player has a ball inside a designated area about twenty yards by twenty yards. Everyone tries to kick everyone's ball out who is on the opposite team. Once your own ball is kicked out you can help your teammates by getting open for a pass within the area or try to kick the ball out from someone of the opposite team. The team with the last remaining ball is declared the winner.

Variation
Select two or three players from each team who are only defenders and try to take the balls away from everyone on the opposite team. Players who have the ball may not take a ball away from another player and once their own ball is kicked out may only receive a pass.

Coaching Tips
This game can go really quickly but by making the square larger you can make it last longer. Encourage players to act as support by getting into an open space.

Race, Pass, Score

Skills
Getting to the ball first
Getting into the open space
Passing

Drill Description
Have the team stand behind the coach who has a pile of soccer balls at his feet. The coach picks up one ball and drop kicks it out in any direction (or simply kicks it) and calls out two names. The two players whose names were called race to the ball and try to get to it first. The first one to the ball takes control of it and turns it towards the coach. The second player stops racing to the ball as soon as the first player gets to it and moves into an open space for a pass. The pair then passes back and forth two or three times before passing it back to the coach. Have several pairs going at the same time to create obstacles for each other and to keep the whole group moving. As soon as a pair returns send them out again together or send each person out with a new partner.

Variations
Set up a goal for the pair to shoot on. The first person gets the ball, the second breaks for the goal and for a pass, after receiving the ball he shoots on goal and both follow the shot into the goal. Add a defender after a while.

Send three players out when you kick it and the first person who gets to the ball turns it while the other two break for the goal towards opposite sides of the goal and the player with the ball finds the open player to pass to.

Coaching Tips
This is a great drill to do as a warm up before a game to get players running and to remind them to spread out.

Count to Three and Pass

Skills
Quick passing
Moving to the open space to receive a pass
Passing to the open person

Drill Description
Divide the group into two teams and play a regular soccer game with
two goals, only in this game players are only allowed to touch the ball
for the count of three before they have to pass it. If a player touches it
more for more than the count of three they have to go over to the side
of the field in a pre-designated area and do a quick exercise (jumping
jacks, sit ups, etc.) before retuning to the game.

Variation
Instead of counting to three allow players to only have three touches
on the ball before they must pass it.

Coaching Tips
A really good player will automatically look around for someone to
pass to or for room to dribble or shoot when a ball is being passed to
her. Younger players usually do not do this but it can still be taught and
hopefully be picked up later. This drill is good for a team with a few
"ball hogs" who don't pass and keep the ball to themselves even when
defenders are on them and to encourage players to pass to an open
player.

Go the Right Direction

Skill
Learning Field Orientation

Drill Description
When young children first play soccer they sometimes have a hard time remembering which way to go when playing an actual game. This activity is a fun way to help them learn about the field. First, show the team the entire field and name all of the sections and lines on the field (i.e. goal line, goal box, near touchline, far touchline, offensive goal, defensive goal, etc.). After going over the field and identifying all the sections and lines, play the following game. Gather the team together and yell, "skip to the near touchline" or "hop to the nearest goal box" or "spin to the defensive goal," etc. Once everyone makes it to the designated area, call out a new area. You can do this drill with or without the soccer ball.

Coaching Tips
This drill is best for younger players who get confused and go the wrong way down the field during the game.

Subtraction Soccer

Skills
Getting to the ball first

Drill Description
Place all of the available soccer balls in the middle, divide the group into two teams and have them start on opposite goal lines. On the "go" signal have the groups race toward the center line and try to get as many balls as possible and take them through the opposite goal for a point. Count how many goals each team scores after each round and then have them place all of the balls back into the middle. Do this several times and take one ball away each time you start until there is only one ball left.

Variation
In order to score a point, the ball must be dribbled to the opposite line and stopped on the line.

Coaching Tips
Have players return balls to the middle after each round and count how long it takes them to get all the balls and challenge them to beat their best time. Encourage players to gain control of a ball and to not take a wild swipe at any ball when going after it against others.

Get Ready!

Skills
Setting up quickly for a free kick, throw-in, goal kick, or corner kick

Drill Description
Divide the group into two teams and designate one team to be offense
and one team to be defense. Walk around the field with a ball and set
it down somewhere and call "free kick", "corner kick", etc. depending
on where you are standing. The two teams race to get into position.
The defense should be marking individual players and guarding the
goal while the offensive players should be moving into the open space
or set up in the correct position to receive a kick. Give one "point"
to the first team to set up in the correct positions before picking up
the ball and moving to another place. Halfway through the drill have
teams switch from offense to defense and defense to offense.

Variation
Set up a very small soccer field, so that the ball will go out often when
a game is played. Every time the ball goes out ask the players where it
is they should be for the corner kick, throw-in, goal kick, etc. and have
the players go to the right spots before sending the ball back into play.

Coaching Tips
This drill works best with one coach or parent assigned to each team to
tell that team where to stand for each situation. Keep this drill moving
by quickly changing from one situation to another.

Square Keep Away

Skills
Passing to the open space
Making accurate passes

Drill Description
This game is just like keep away with one person in the middle and
two players on each side who pass back and forth trying to keep the
ball away from the person in the middle; only in this game the two
players have safety squares they can stand in. The person in the middle
cannot go into the squares but can get the ball at any time when it is
outside the square. After playing like this for a while, change the drill
so that there are four squares instead of two, with one person in the
middle and three on the outside. The players in the squares can move
to an empty square to create support for the person with the ball. After
a while, change the drill to regular 'keep away' where there are no
safety zones but still with three keeping away from one.

Variation
Play a game of 'keep away' with one person in the middle of the
square. The player in the middle cannot leave the square and those on
the outside have to pass though the square to their teammates.

Coaching Tips
The squares help younger players practice passing to the open space
without the pressure of a defender taking the ball away and without
the defender always getting the ball. Make the square big enough for
players to move from side to side in order to get around the defender.
A player can dribble out of the square at any time to get around
a defender as well. When playing the four square game, focus on
moving to the open space.

Shooting

Many young players, when they first start playing, will play on a small field with small goals and possibly with no goalie. For this type of play, a pass or a low hard kick are needed for scoring a goal. As players get older and the field gets bigger, being able to shoot the ball with accuracy and power becomes more important.

Young players can easily form bad habits if they continually shoot using improper form. Thus it is good to try to teach them proper shooting form at a young age. Many young players will kick with the end of their toe, which is hard to control. Others will not look at the ball when making contact with it and will miss the ball completely when shooting. Another common mistake is for the body to be too close to the ball when the player strikes it, and no power can be put into the shot.

The important aspects of a good shot on goal include foot placement, foot posture, and striking the ball in the right place. The ball should be hit with the top part of the foot (or the laces of the shoe). You can come at the ball straight on or from an angle. For more power the shooter should step into the shot. For young players, I use the "flick it and kick it" technique. They give the ball a little flick out in front of them and then step into the shot and kick it. Another technique for teaching shooting is to have players practice drop kicks against a fence, wall, or backstop. When executing a drop kick they should have their toe pointed down and the ankle locked. This is also the position the foot should be in when taking a shot. The way the knee snaps during a drop kick will also help give players the feel for how a powerful shot should feel with a knee snap and follow through. Players should briefly look up at the target before shooting, but look at the ball when making contact with it. To get the ball to go up in the air the ball should be struck in the lower half. Significantly, for the younger ages, discourage using the toe as a primary way of shooting the ball.

Shooting Drills

Gate Choice

Skills
Dribbling
Shooting
Choosing the open space

Drill Description
The group lines up on the center line and each individual has a ball.
Set up two gates with cones; one on the right and one on the left (in
front of the goal). The coach stands in-between the gates and calls one
player's name. That player dribbles down and must choose a gate to go
through before shooting on goal. The coach jumps into one gate and
the player should choose the other gate and go through it.

Coaching Tips
This is a great drill to start showing players the importance of choosing
the open space. If you have more than one coach you can do this drill
in smaller groups to eliminate the amount of time players wait in line.

Sweatshirt Target

Skills
Kicking the ball up in the air and off the ground.

Drill Description
Most schools and parks have a backstop for baseball. Bring a sweatshirt with a picture on it such as a Mickey Mouse sweatshirt. Hang the sweatshirt on the backstop a few feet off of the ground, by sticking the arms through the fence. Challenge the team to hit the target by kicking the ball into the picture on the shirt.

Coaching Tips
This is a good drill for shooting practice and especially for making shots higher, off the ground. Players have more fun shooting at a target, but watch out for any player running to get her ball while others are shooting. And of course remind players not to kick with their toes!

Quick Shot

Skills
Making quick, accurate shots on goal

Drill Description
Have the team gather up all of the balls and place them somewhere on the line that marks the outside of the goal box (or make a line out of cones). Select one player to be the shooter and give this player thirty seconds to shoot as many of the balls as he can within the time period. The rest of the team is behind the goal gathering up the balls and counting how many goals the shooter makes. You may or may not have a goalie for this drill. After thirty seconds, count to ten and cheer the children on as they set up the balls on the line again and challenge them to get them all set up for the next shooter by the count of ten.

Variation
Have everyone get a ball and place it on the goal box line, but spread out from their teammates. Place a goalie in the goal and quickly call out one name at a time. When a player's name is called, he must take a shot as quickly as possible. After everyone has taken a shot, give them to the count of ten to quickly gather up the balls and put them back on the line in a new spot for the next round.

Coaching Tips
Keep this drill moving quickly so that those not shooting are still involved. Watch for toe kicks and remind players how to shoot properly by hitting the ball with the laces, with knee bent and ankle locked down.

Shooting Drills

Breakaway

Skills
Keeping the ball in control during a breakaway towards the goal

Drill Description
Players line up in a two single file lines at the center of the field one yard apart, facing the goal. Each person has a ball. The coach yells "go" and the first person in each line dribbles as quickly as she can toward the goal and then takes a shot on goal. Set up a cone line that they must pass before taking a shot. This can be done with or without a goalie. The coach gives one point at his discretion to any player who keeps the ball in control when dribbling and one point for each goal that is scored and one point to the player who scores first.

Variations
To prevent players from over dribbling and losing control of the ball, set up a box where players must be inside when they shoot.

Players in one line dribble and try to score while players in the other line (who do not have a ball) act as a defender when you say, "go." The defender line might be placed slightly behind the other line.

Have one player go at time and simply give points for goals made.

Coaching Tips
Younger players often lose control of the ball when they are in break away situations and even though they have an open goal they'll miss the entire goal or kick it over the end line before having a chance to shoot. This drill helps them practice getting a shot on goal. Encourage players to shoot on goal when close enough to make a goal. Young players like to hear the coach tell them how many points they received after each attempt. In the end nobody will be able to keep track of the total number of points, which is a good thing.

Targets and Numbers

Skills
Look up at target before kicking ball
Kicking accuracy
Being aware of what's going on around you while dribbling

Drill Description
Set up a target to be kicked at (i.e., a cone, box, etc.). Players get into a single file line facing the target, though at least twenty feet away. The first few rounds of this drill the players take turns dribbling for a few feet and then kicking at the target, trying to hit it. Afterward the coach stands near the target and holds up one or two fingers and each person must yell out the number of fingers the coach is holding up before kicking at the target. Once the children get good at this, challenge them to hit a moving target (the coach) who walks back and forth.

Coaching Tips
When making contact with the ball, players should look at the ball; however, as noted, they should look at the target right before kicking.

Give a Ball

Skills
Receiving a pass in front of the goal and taking a quick shot on goal

Drill Description
Half the team stands on the right side of the goal just outside the penalty box and the other half of the team stands on the left side. Each player has a ball. Select one person to be the first shooter and he stands in front of the goal at the edge of the goal box. The shooter calls one person at a time and this individual can either kick his ball or use a throw-in to get their ball to the shooter, who takes it and shoots the ball quickly before calling for a ball from anther player. Switch off players so everyone gets a chance taking quick shots on goal.

Variation
If you have a large group, it might be better to divide them into smaller groups for this drill and set up a goal for each group.

Coaching Tips
Quick shots should be taken after the player traps the ball and moves it slightly in front of himself. At this age lots of players kick with their toe and need to be told time and time again to kick with the proper part of the foot. Also players form the bad habit of backing up before taking a shot, rather than stepping into the shot or tapping it out in front before shooting.

Quick Dribble, Quick Shot!

Skills
Dribbling quickly
Shooting quickly within a small space

Drill Description
Use one half of a field that has a soccer goal for this drill. Five yards
on each side of the goal set up a line of cones that players must dribble
in and out of, doing so in a large arc out into the field and back toward
the goal. Each side will have a line of players racing through the cones
against the other side. After the line of cones arcs back toward the
goal, make a box using four cones at the outer edge of the penalty area.
When the coach says "go," the two players in the front of each line
race against each other through the cones and into the box where they
take a shot on goal. Give one point to the first person to take a shot
inside the box and one point to any player who scores a goal. (Nobody
really knows how many points they accumulate during this game, but
they like to hear how many points they get each round.) Have players
switch lines each time. This drill can be done with or without a goalie.

Coaching Tips
Using the shooting box in this drill will really help players take quick
shots. At times I have had players who will back up before shooting to
set things up, and when this happens, I announce that anyone who does
this gets zero points. Players who back up give the other team time to
take the ball away from them before they can shoot. To get the ball set
up for a shot without backing up, encourage the "flick it and kick it"
technique.

Running Shooting Running

Skills
Shooting after a break away run

Drill Description
Use a mini soccer field, full field, or set up two goals to make your
own field. The coach and the assistant coach start out as goalies, with
one in each goal (or have a player be goalie at one end and the coach
at the other). Everyone starts at the coach's goal with a ball. The coach
calls out the name of one person at a time, who takes a shot on goal.
The shooter then retrieves his own ball before dribbling down to the
other end where he shoots on that goal; after shooting on the second
goal, each player dribbles back down to shoot on the coach, and so
on, back and forth until the coach calls "stop." Make a big deal about
having them count how many times they scored, and for a reward give
a water break after every three goals.

Coaching Tips
As a goalie, don't try as hard to stop shots from weaker players; then
everyone gets a water break at about the same time. My players really
like this drill and have fun running and running even when it seems
like they would want to quit.

Fun Soccer Drills that Teach Soccer Skills

Throw-ins

Since there are so many other skills you will need to work on with your team, throw-ins are something you won't spend a lot of time working on at practice. However, moving the ball back into play quickly and accurately can be a great advantage. The main points to teach when working on throw-ins are the rules of a proper throw-in, the direction where the throw should go, and accuracy of the throw.

The biggest rule infraction that takes place during a throw-in occurs when the foot is lifted off of the ground during the throw. At the younger ages the referee will often allow the player to retake the throw when this occurs but at the older ages the other team will be given the throw. During the throw-in drills, emphasize that both feet stay on the ground when the ball is released; otherwise the throw doesn't count (as far as the drill goes). This helps young players get used to keeping both feet on the ground.

When taking a throw-in, it is also important to throw the ball in the direction your team is going and not back toward the defense or in the middle of the field when on your defensive end. Throwing the ball down the sideline toward the goal, you are shooting on is the easiest way to teach young players to not throw it in a danger area. Of course your team must get open and be ready to receive a ball in this location as well. Finding a teammate who is close enough for the thrower to hit their feet with the ball is the ideal place to aim for.

Taking a quick throw can give your team an advantage as well. This prevents the other team from moving into the defensive position too quickly.

With very young teams you may run into the problem of players fighting over the ball when it goes out of bounds and everyone wanting to throw. A couple of ways to deal with this problem are to assign one person to take all throws and kicks for one round of play (this works OK when the games are three vs. three), or you can allow the person closest to the ball when it goes out to take the throw.

Throw-in Drills

Moving Coach Target

Skills
Throwing in to a moving target

Drill Description
Each player lines up on the sideline with a ball. The coach runs down the field and everyone throws in to try and hit the coach in the feet while she is running. After throwing in, the kids should run to get their ball and run to the other sideline for another round of throw-ins. Go back and forth a few times to keep them moving.

Variation
Have them throw-in one at a time and run onto the field toward the goal for a pass from the coach and then take a shot on goal.

Coaching Tips
Younger players think it is fun to do anything where they get to go after the coach. The more dramatic you are about being hit the more fun the players have with this drill. Emphasize proper throw-ins with both feet on the ground and keeping both hands on the ball when throwing.

Target Throw-in

Skills
Throw-in to partner's feet

Drill Description
For this activity you need a swing set to be near your practice area. Since most practices for this age group take place on school grounds or at a park, there should be a swing set near.

Divide the group into pairs and give each pair one ball. After going over the proper technique for how to throw-in, go over to a swing set and have one partner stand on each side of a swing but a few feet back. Challenge the group to throw through the chains of the swing and to hit their partner's feet with the ball. Each person should take turns practicing their throw-ins to her partner.

Variation
Find other places around the practice field with places to throw-in.

Coaching Tips
Younger players need to be reminded continually to keep both feet on the ground when making a throw-in and to throw with two hands on the ball.

Coach Throw-in

Skills
Moving to the open space when your team has a throw-in
Marking the other team when their team has a throw-in

Drill Description
Make a small soccer field or use your usual practice field size. Two coaches or parents are needed for this drill. Divide the group into two teams and tell the players which goal they are shooting at. The two coaches are on opposite sides of the field, each with a pile of balls. One coach will yell "my throw-in" and his team has to quickly move into position to receive a throw-in and the other team must defend by individually marking these players. After throwing the ball in, the two teams play regular soccer until one team scores, the ball goes out, or either coach yells "my throw-in" -- at which point the ball in play should be kicked out and everyone runs into position for another throw-in. Either coach can throw-in at anytime, and can even throw two in a row.

Coaching Tips
Talk to the team about moving to an open space that is toward the goal they are shooting on and up their own sideline. Throw-ins should not be thrown directly into the middle of the field or toward the teams own goal because the other team will have a better chance of taking the ball and shooting on goal.

Throw-in Challenge

Skills
Making accurate throw-ins
Being able to make a long throw-in

Drill Description
Make a sideline using cones or use an existing sideline on your practice field. Set up one cone in the field about one yard away. Set up a second cone two yards out (one yard behind the first) and then another one three yards out. Players line up on the sideline in a single file line facing the cones and each player has a ball. Each player takes a turn taking a throw-in and tries to hit the first cone. Players go to the end of the line after each try. After hitting the first cone a player then tries for the second cone when it is his turn again. Challenge players to be the first one to hit the third cone. There can be several lines of this going on at once, with only two or three players in each line.

Variations
Make this a relay race. Each time a player on one team hits a cone, he can grab that cone and place it on top of the next cone and this becomes the target for the whole team until a player hits it. The first team to hit all of the cones wins.

For an additional challenge, add more cones or space the cones further apart.

Coaching Tips
This is a great drill to have set up when players arrive to practice and can join in. Only count cones as a hit when one is hit by a properly taken throw-in. Players can get good exercise running after each throw-in taken, before getting back in line, which is another good reason to have this set up as a warm up drill when practice begins.

Throw-in Dodge Ball

Skills
Accurate Throw-ins

Drill Description
Divide the group into two teams. Set up a line using cones with one team on one side of the line and one on the other. Spread out as many balls as you have into the field as well. On the "go" signal players can pick up any ball and make a throw-in to the other side without crossing the line. If a player on the other team is hit below the knees, she must go to the other team. To count, the throw-in must be a legal throw-in with both feet on the ground. The game ends when everyone is on one side.

Variation
Set up a line behind each team and if a player is hit she goes to the line you have set up behind the opposite team and waits for one of her teammates to throw-in to her feet (or kick it) so she can trap it and dribble back to her side. The first team to get everyone else on the other team "out" at the same time wins.

Coaching Tips
Adjust the rules if players want to go back to their original side and wait for their old teammates to get them 'out'.

Fun Soccer Drills that Teach Soccer Skills

Alphabetical List of Drills

Other Books by Alanna Jones

104 Activities That Build:
Self-Esteem, Teamwork, Communication, Anger Management, Self-Discovery, and Coping Skills
This popular book makes teaching and learning by playing games a simple and fun experience for everyone.

Team-Building Activities for Every Group
107 interactive games and activities can be found in the pages of this easy-to-use book. Each game is fun, experiential, easy to lead, unique, and requires minimal resources.

More Team-Building Activities for Every Group
This book contains 107 more games and activities that promote team-building in an interactive and fun way. The games are new, different, experiential, exciting, easy to lead and require minimal resources.

Therapy Games: Creative Ways to Turn Popular Games Into Activities That Build Self-Esteem, Communication Skills, Anger Management, Self-Discovery, and Coping Skills
In this book you will find 102 new and exciting ways to turn ordinary games into Therapy Games

---

To find sample games from each of these books and order information
visit www.gamesforgroups.com

For more information or to order the book
Fun Soccer Drills that Teach Soccer Skills to 5, 6, 7 year olds
visit www.gamesforsoccer.com